A Healthcare Economic Policy for Hearing Impairment

Artem Boltyenkov

A Healthcare Economic Policy for Hearing Impairment

Foreword by Prof. Dr. Arnis Vilks

Springer Gabler

Artem Boltyenkov
Leipzig, Germany

Dissertation, HHL – Leipzig Graduate School of Management, 2014

ISBN 978-3-658-08236-9 ISBN 978-3-658-08237-6 (eBook)
DOI 10.1007/978-3-658-08237-6

Library of Congress Control Number: 2014956554

Springer Gabler

Printed on acid-free paper

Springer Gabler is a brand of Springer Fachmedien Wiesbaden
Springer Fachmedien Wiesbaden is part of Springer Science+Business Media
(www.springer.com)

Foreword

More than 200 million people around the world are suffering from hearing impairment, with the majority living in developing countries. In most cases hearing impairment means more or less complete exclusion from the hearing society, and seriously diminished opportunities to earn an income in particular. While, again in most cases, a suitable hearing aid could remedy the situation considerably, and at relatively low cost, it is estimated that less than 3% of those who would need a hearing aid actually have one.

Artem Boltyenkov, who has been working in the hearing aid industry for many years, has done a through study of the situation, looking at the problem of hearing impairment from all conceivable angles, but with the ultimate aim of assessing the different possibilities to finance hearing aids. Based on dozens of interviews and 250 responses to a comprehensive questionnaire, he has identified the main factors that contribute to the usefulness and acceptance of hearing aids, and he has analysed thoroughly how a limited budget for subsidies could best be used to make such hearing aids affordable to those who need them. The study fills a noticeable gap in the literature and deserves the attention of health-care policy makers around the world.

Leipzig

Prof. Dr. Arnis Vilks
Professor of Economics
HHL – Leipzig Graduate School of Management

Preface

This research explores the ways in which the hearing impaired can afford aided hearing. The focus is on Ukraine and Russia, but the findings can be applied to other developing countries. In Ukraine, only some groups of the hearing impaired have access to free government hearing aids. In Russia, the situation is similar but not the same. There, the hearing impaired have access to partial reimbursement. The research analyses the possibilities of improvement the current healthcare policies in Ukraine and in Russia.

The research method used in the study is the grounded theory approach.[1] It is based on empirical research with the quantitative verification of the newly formed theory via Confirmatory Factor Analysis. To conceptualize the theory, the author conducted a series of interviews with the hearing impaired, consumer finance experts, hearing aid dispensers, hearing instrument and implant manufacturers, non-government organizations and other experts. All this has allowed to formulate the hypothesis on an alternative healthcare economic policy for hearing impairment. A formal survey for hearing impaired people was developed. It measures their hearing loss, daily activities, occupation, quality of life, access to reimbursement and other indicators. The survey was conducted mostly in the USA, Russia and Ukraine. Subsequently, the survey results were analyzed with Confirmatory Factor Analysis to refine and confirm the findings of the qualitative research.

The first finding of the study is that not all hearing impaired will equally benefit from aided hearing. The hearing impaired who often need to use their hearing ability while speaking on the phone, holding a conversation in areas with a lot of background noise, participating in group discussions or talking with strangers will gain the most. Least of all will benefit the hearing impaired who are fully integrated in the deaf society, and those who communicate with normal-hearing people only occasionally in one-on-one conversations. The hearing impaired with high income, who have a high subjective time-value-of-money discount rate and access to at least partial reimbursement, are in better position to afford aided hearing though savings. On the other hand, the hearing impaired who are satisfied with their prior aided hearing experience, willing to borrow money and put up some of their assets as collateral, are best positioned to afford aided hearing through borrowing.

The most humane option for all hearing impaired is full reimbursement healthcare economic policy. Unfortunately, providing free aided hearing for all

---

1 Glaser & Strauss, 1967.

hearing impaired in the population is very costly. Countries, which cannot afford such generosity, need to know how to spend their limited resources wisely. We recommend implementing the subsidized loans or the subsidized savings and loans healthcare economic policy to help the hearing impaired to afford aided hearing.

The best solution for person's hearing loss is the one that meets the needs of the hearing impaired at an affordable price. We show that the subsidized savings and loans policy allows all hearing impaired, regardless of their wealth, to get access to aided hearing. Besides, in this research, we show that the subsidized loans policy is more cost-effective than the partial lump-sum reimbursement currently used in Russia and other countries. Partial lump-sum reimbursement policy often leads to over-reimbursing people, who can afford aided hearing without any external help, and to under-reimbursing people, who cannot afford aided hearing even with the partial lump-sum reimbursement.

Dr. Artem Boltyenkov

Table of Contents

List of Figures

List of Tables

List of Abbreviations

AGIF	–	Adjusted Goodness of Fit
ADF	–	Asymptotic Distribution Free
BAHA	–	Bone anchored hearing aid
BiCROS	–	Bilateral Contralateral Routing of Signal
BTE	–	Behind The Ear
CFA	–	Confirmatory Factor Analysis
CFI	–	Comparative Fit Index
CIC	–	Completely In the Canal
CROS	–	Contralateral Routing of Signal
dB	–	Decibel
df	–	Degrees of Freedom
ENT	–	Ear, nose, and throat
GIF	–	Goodness of Fit
HRA	–	Health Reimbursement Account
HSA	–	Healthcare Savings Account
Hz	–	Hertz
IIC	–	Invisible In the Canal
IOI-HA	–	International Outcome Inventory for Hearing Aids
ITC	–	In The Canal
ITE	–	In The Ear
kHz	–	Kilohertz
ML	–	Maximum Likelihood
mm	–	Millimeter
ms	–	Millisecond
MFI	–	Microfinance Institution
MSA	–	Medical Savings Account
OTE	–	Over The Ear
PGIF	–	Parsimony Goodness of Fit
QALY	–	Quality Adjusted Life Years

RITE	–	Receiver In The Ear
RMR	–	Root Mean square Residual
RMSEA	–	Root Mean Square Error of Approximation
ROSCA	–	Rotating Saving and Credit Association
SADL	–	Satisfaction in Amplification in Daily Life
TLI	–	Tucker-Lewis Index
UK	–	United Kingdom
USA	–	United States of America
USD	–	United States Dollar
WLS	–	Weighted Least Squares
YLD	–	Years Lived with Disability

1 Introduction

The overwhelming majority of activities we do in our everyday life involves communication with other people with the help of speech.

> "Impaired hearing results in distorted or incomplete communication leading to greater isolation and withdrawal and therefore lower sensory input. In turn, the individual's life space and social life becomes restricted. One could logically think that a constricted lifestyle would negatively impact the psychosocial well-being of people with hearing loss." [1]

In addition, it prevents them from fully participating in social life activities. Hearing loss creates such health problems as

> "... embarrassment, fatigue, irritability, tension and stress, avoidance of social activities, withdrawal from social situations, depression, negativism, danger to personal safety, rejection by others, reduced general health, loneliness, social isolation, less alertness to the environment, paranoia, lessened ability to cope and reduced overall psychological health. In view of this, few would disagree that hearing loss *per se* is a serious issue." [2]

Many of the conditions associated with hearing loss are of physiological nature.

> "The tragedy is that untreated hearing loss impacts the individual and his or her family for the rest of his or her life in the form of lost wages, lost promotions, lost opportunities, and unrealized dreams, not to mention lower income in their retirement." [3]

In 2013, the World Health Organization estimated that there are around 360 million people worldwide with moderate to profound hearing impairment.[4] While there are many causes of hearing loss, including genetic factors, ageing, disease, trauma, and exposure to excessively loud noise, the most common treatment for an individual suffering from hearing loss is the use of hearing instruments or implants. "Half of all cases of hearing loss are avoidable through primary prevention".[5] Another alarming finding of World Health Organization is the following:

---

1 Kochkin, 2013, p. 1.
2 Kochkin & Rogin, 2000, p. 10.
3 Kochkin, 2005, p. 9.
4 World Health Organization, 2013.
5 World Health Organization, 2013, p. 1.

> "In developing countries, fewer than one out of 40 people who need a hearing aid have one. The lack of availability of services for fitting and maintaining hearing aids, and the lack of batteries are also barriers in many low-income settings." [6]

With this research, we want to find a better healthcare economic policy to help the hearing impaired to afford a hearing instrument or an implant, increase the number of aided hearing impaired, and help more hearing impaired to become economically active members of society. On December 13, 2006 United Nation adopted the Convention on the Rights of Persons with Disabilities. One of the main guiding principles of the Convention is the full and effective participation and inclusion of disabled in society.

> "If development is about bringing excluded people into society, then disabled people belong in schools, legislatures, at work, on buses, at the theatre and everywhere else that those who aren't disabled take for granted. Unless disabled people are brought into the development mainstream, it will be impossible to cut poverty in half by 2015 or to give every boy or girl the chance to achieve a primary education by the same date, goals agreed to by more than 180 world leaders at the United Nations Millennium Summit in September, 2000." [7]

6 World Health Organization, 2013, pp. 5-6.

7 Wolfensohn, 2002.

2 Background

2.1 The Hearing Sense

People hear by detecting sounds vibration. Hearing is one of the five senses (sight, hearing, taste, smell, and touch) that humans possess.

The human ear consists of the outer ear, the middle ear, and the inner ear (Figure 1). The outer ear can be further split into pinna, concha, external auditory meatus (ear canal), and ear drum. The middle ear is located behind the ear drum and consists of three ossicles (malleus, incus, stapes), which transmit vibration of the eardrum into vibrations of the oval window membrane. The oval window membrane is the point of entrance for sound vibration from the middle ear to the inner ear. The inner ear consists of cochlear and vestibular system. The cochlear is responsible for conversion of vibration to electrical signals that are communicated via neurotransmitters to many thousands of nerve cells. Then the neurons transform the electric signals into electrochemical impulses, which travel along the auditory nerve to structures in the brainstem for further processing.

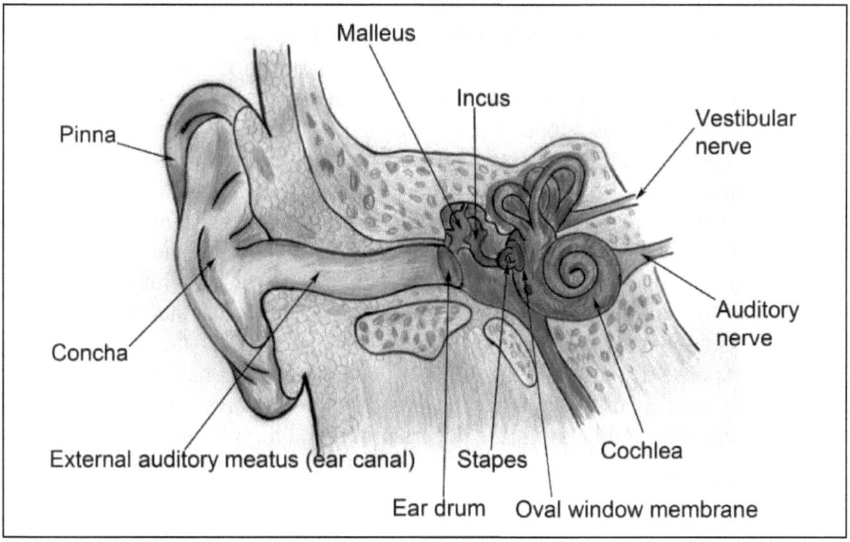

Figure 1: Anatomy of the Human Ear.

The pinna and the outer third of the ear canal are internally made of the elastic cartilage and are different for different individuals. The bony part forms the inner two thirds of the ear canal. The ear canal is typically "S" shaped with a diameter of a pencil and a length of 25 to 30 mm in adults. It has two primary functions. The first function of the outer ear is to protect the ear from external bodies such as dirt, debris, and insects. The second function of the outer ear is to channel sound into the ear. In addition, with the help of the outer ear, direction-dependent deformation of the incoming acoustical signal is performed. It is used for detecting the location of the sound source. This means that if the pinna is chopped off, it will be impossible for the ear to detect the direction from which the sound is coming. The ear canal combined with the pinna effect leads to the gain increase of 15-25 dB (decibel). In this research, gain represents the measure of power increase on a logarithmic scale in dB.

The middle ear is located in the tympanic cavity. The tympanic cavity is filled with air and is connected with the pharynx through the Eustachian tube. During swallowing and yawning the Eustachian tube widens making the atmospheric pressure on both sides of the ear drum equal. The middle ear function is passing and transforming the relatively low impedance[1] of the acoustical waves of the air in the outer ear to the high impedance of fluid in the inner ear. Without this function the big part of the sound energy would be lost during the transformation from air to liquid mediums, which in turn will cause significantly smaller sensitivity of the human ear to sounds. Thus, the middle ear adds about 27 dB of gain to the sound vibrations going from the ear drum to the oval window.

The inner ear consists of the series of canals and cavities filled with fluid. It functions as the organ of hearing and the organ of balance at the same time. The cochlear is the part of the inner ear responsible for hearing. Inside it, there are sensory receptors of auditory system called hair cells. They are located on the basilar membrane, and play a crucial role in sound waves transfer to the brain. The basilar membrane disperses the incoming sound waves to separate frequencies spatially. This means that the sound input of certain frequencies vibrates hair cells in certain locations more than in others. In particular, high frequency sounds lead to maximum vibration at the base of the basilar membrane, while low frequencies result in maximum vibration at the apex of the basilar membrane. In response to vibration, the hair cells release neurotransmitters triggering a nerve impulse. Due to the fact that the sound "wave" always passes through the base first, sensorineural hearing loss occurs initially at high frequencies.

---

1 Impedance is the measure of responsiveness of a medium to vibrations caused by the sound pressure. It is measured as a ratio of sound pressure to particle velocity in a given medium. Low impedance means that it is easy for the sound to travel in the medium. High impedance means that it is difficult.

After a nerve impulse is triggered by hair cells, it travels along the nerve cells passing through different "stops" along the neural pathway. The majority of nerve fibers cross from one side of the brain to the other. This means the right half of the brain processes the sound signals from the left ear, and the left half of the brain processes the sound signals from the right ear. The signal ends in the auditory cortex of the brain, where it is interpreted.

It is important to note that the brain uses input from both ears for optimal processing. Binaural summation of sounds from both ears adds about 3 dB to the resulting sound. Due to the effect of binaural redundancy, the same sound is heard twice, and the brain is better equipped to identify the source of the sound. In addition, hearing with both ears allows understanding speech better, even in noisy environment, because of the binaural noise suppression by the brain. Therefore, in case of hearing loss in both ears, two hearing aids are highly recommended.

2.2 Types and Causes of Hearing Loss

Some hearing impaired people cannot hear any sounds at all. Others can comprehend speech only when shouted close to their ears. There are hearing impaired people who are able to hear some sounds, but not all. This is an especially dangerous situation, as a hearing impaired person might not be aware of her/his impairment. In such a case, she/he attributes her/his lack of speech understanding to the fact that other people in her/his presence mumble or speak unclearly.

Many hearing impaired people with mild to moderate sensorineural hearing loss can hear the vowels but have trouble hearing the consonants.[2] This may lead to a particularly difficult and embarrassing situation for a hearing impaired person: she/he hears the speech, but often misunderstands what is being said. For example: "the sequence of sounds i e a ar, might have originated as pick the black harp, but could be heard as kick the cat hard."[3] As can be seen from this example, simply amplifying the sound at all frequencies at the same amplification will not help a hearing impaired person to understand the speech correctly; it might just make the wrong acoustical information sound louder. A correctly fitted hearing instrument outputs the acoustical information in such a way and at such frequencies that it enables a hearing impaired person to understand correctly what is being said. Therefore, a hearing instrument needs to be individually adjusted to the hearing loss profile.

---

2 Macrae & Dillon, 1996.

3 Dillon, 2001, p.2.

An audiogram is a standard way of representing a person's hearing loss profile. Audiograms show frequency of sounds in speech on the horizontal axis, typically on the logarithmic scale, in hertz (Hz). Intensity of sound, or simply put loudness[4], is presented on the vertical axis on the linear scale in decibels (dB). On an audiogram, one can clearly see the degree of hearing loss at each frequency.

There are two main types of audiograms. They are the air conduction audiogram and the bone conduction audiogram. The former shows the hearing loss measured when the sound travels all the way from the outer ear, through the middle ear to the inner ear. It demonstrates the performance of the patient's whole hearing system in one of the ears. As a rule, loudspeakers or earphones are used for air conduction testing.

The bone conduction audiogram shows the hearing loss in the inner ear. A bone vibrator is used for bone conduction testing. It is placed behind the ear to send vibrations directly to a patient's skull. Those vibrations bypass the outer and the middle ears, and are directly transformed into movements of the hair cells on the basilar membrane. This makes it possible to measure the hearing loss precisely in the cochlear.

The air and the bone conduction audiograms help to determine the type of hearing loss a patient suffers from. In the diagrams of the figures, the solid line represents an air conduction audiogram; the dashed line is a bone conduction audiogram.

The audiogram in Figure 2 shows normal hearing. A person with normal hearing has no difficulty in speech understanding.

The audiogram in Figure 3 shows a mild hearing loss. A person with this hearing loss may have difficulty understanding very quiet speech in noisy environment, or distant speech.

4 Although loudness is shown on the linear scale in dB, the measure of sound loudness itself (dB) is a logarithmic unit.

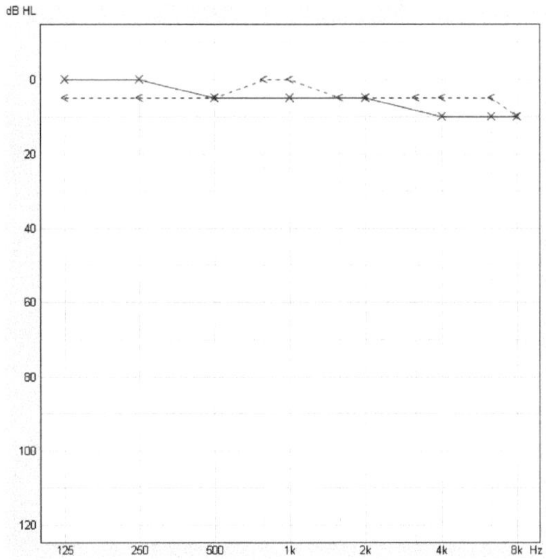

Figure 2: Normal hearing.[5]

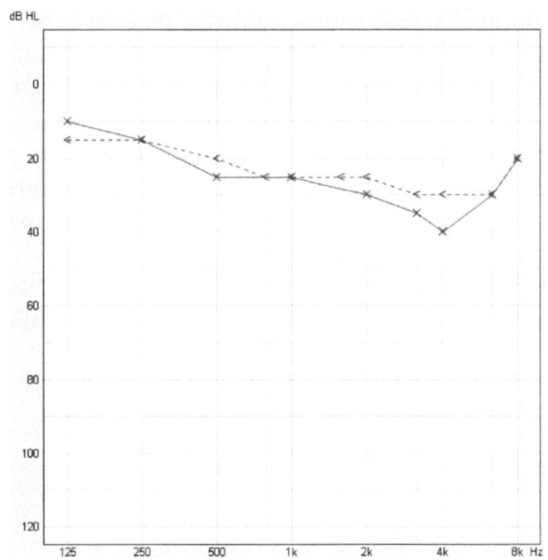

Figure 3: Mild hearing loss.[6]

5 Own illustration using Connexx 6.5.

6 Own illustration using Connexx 6.5.

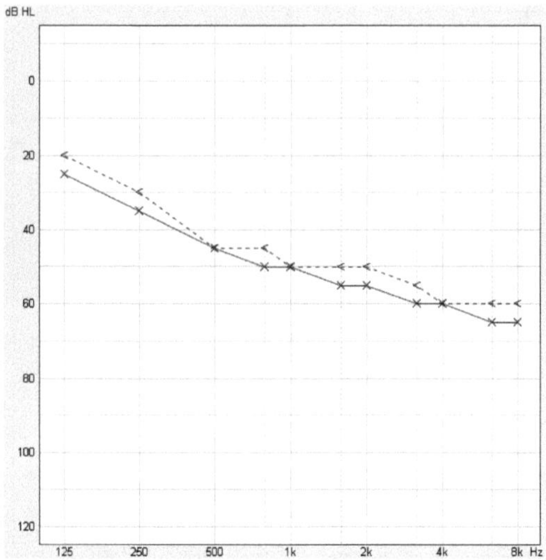

Figure 4: Moderate hearing loss.[7]

The audiogram in Figure 4 shows moderate hearing loss. With this hearing loss, a person understands conversation only at a distance of no more than 3 meters. In areas with background noise a person does not comprehend up to 50% of speech.

The audiogram in Figure 5 shows severe hearing loss. In case of this hearing loss, conversation must be loud to be heard without amplification. A person is aware of loud voices about 30 cm from the ear without amplification but most likely to rely on vision for communication.

The audiogram in Figure 6 shows profound hearing loss. In this case, a person is unable to understand speech even with the help of amplification.

---

7 Own illustration using Connexx 6.5.

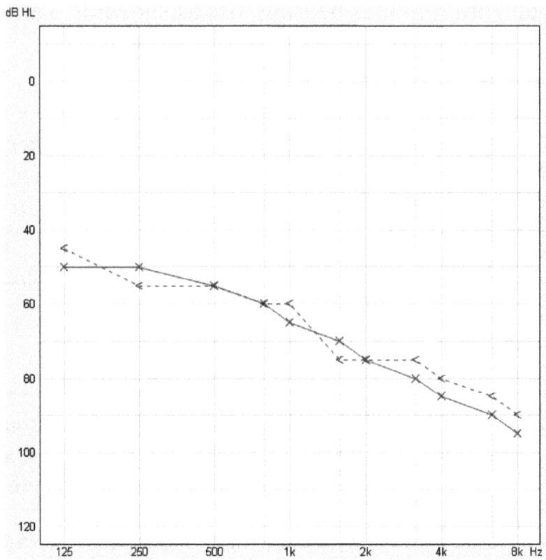

Figure 5: Severe hearing loss.[8]

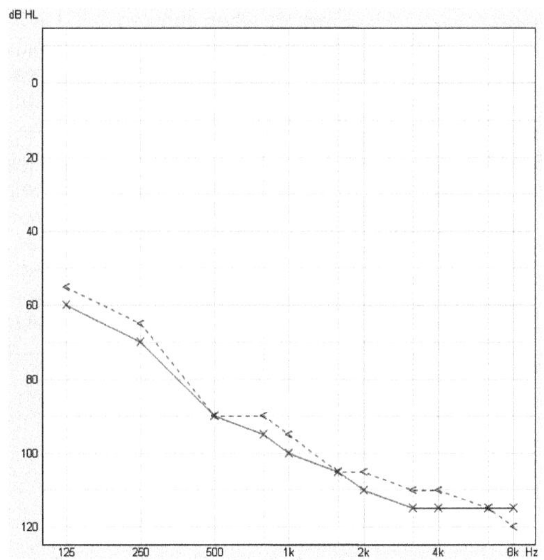

Figure 6: Profound hearing loss.[9]

8 Own illustration using Connexx 6.5.

9 Own illustration using Connexx 6.5.

World Health Organization grades hearing loss as shown in Table 1.

Table 1: Table of grades of hearing impairment.[10]

Grade of impairment	Corresponding audiometric ISO value (Average of 500, 1000, 2000, 4000 Hz)	Performance	Reccomendations
0 **No impairment**	**25 dB or better** (better ear)	No or very slight hearing problems. Able to hear whispers.	
1 **Slight impairment**	**26–40 dB** (better ear)	Able to hear and repeat words spoken in normal voice at 1 metre.	Counselling. Hearing aids may be needed.
2 **Moderate impairment**	**41–60 dB** (better ear)	Able to hear and repeat words using raised voice at 1 metre.	Hearing aids usually recommended.
3 **Severe impairment**	**61–80 dB** (better ear)	Able to hear some words when shouted into better ear.	Hearing aids needed. If no hearing aids available, lip-reading and signing should be taught.
4 **Profound impairment Including deafness**	**81 dB or greater** (better ear)	Unable to hear and understand even a shouted voice.	Hearing aids may help understanding words. Additional rehabilitation needed. Lip-reading and sometimes signing essential.

10 World Health Organization, (1991), p. 2.

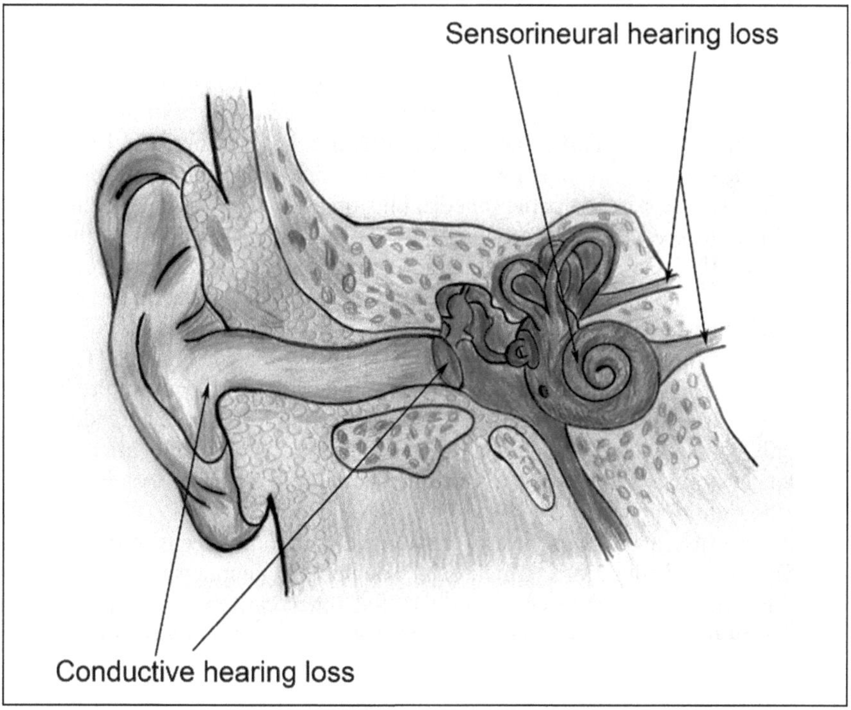

Figure 7: Hearing loss.

Due to the complexity of the hearing organ and the mechanisms used for transferring the sound from the environment to the brain, various disruptions on the way may result in hearing loss. There are three main types of hearing loss (Figure 7):

- Conductive hearing loss. Typically caused by the middle ear infections or malformations.
- Sensorineural hearing loss. Typically caused by the damage of the inner ear and/or the inner cells, or by the damage of the neural structures.
- Mixed hearing loss. A combination of conductive and sensorineural hearing loss.

Conductive hearing loss occurs when the conduction of sound waves from the outer ear to the inner one does not work properly. The problem in conducting sound waves from the outer to the middle ear is most often caused by excess of ear wax, debris in the ear or tumor. Excessive ear wax often, not always though, can be removed with the proper cleaning procedure. Besides, malformations of the pinna and the ear canal may also lead to the blockage and conductive hearing loss. Moreover, disruptions of sound transfer in the middle ear result in conductive hearing loss. These disruptions may occur due to punctures in the ear drum, inflammations of the middle ear such as otitis media, dysfunctional Eustachian tube etc. It is possible to diagnose sound wave conduction problems mentioned above via the analysis of a patient medical history, otoscopy, or/and via the analysis of the difference between audiograms of the air conduction and the bone conduction. If an ear shows hearing loss at the air conduction audiogram, and no hearing loss at the bone conduction audiogram, this means a patient has conductive hearing loss.

In most cases, conductive hearing loss may be treated by an ENT doctor, who can clean the outer ear, or with the help of drugs, like, for example, in case of the otitis media. In rare cases, a surgery is required. Therefore, individuals with only conductive hearing loss are rarely in need of a hearing instrument or an implant. It is always important to diagnose the type of hearing loss in order to select the right treatment.

In case of sensorineural hearing loss, the disruption happens at the point of transformation of vibrations, which enter cochlear, to neural patterns of excitation. The disruption may occur either in the inner ear, the vestibulocochlear nerve, or in the brain itself. Due to the fact that the exact differentiation between these three points of disruption is not possible, hearing loss associated with the sound sensation is called sensorineural hearing loss. Sensorineural hearing loss can range from mild to severe, and even can result in profound deafness. It is about four times more prevalent than conductive hearing loss.

Most often, sensorineural hearing loss is caused by malfunction of hair cells on the basilar membrane. The hair cells may be either damaged at birth or during life of an individual. Frequently, the causes for hair cells damage are trauma, disease, exposure to loud noise, aging or deafness genes. In such cases of sensorineural hearing loss, common treatments are hearing instruments or implants. The main reason for that is inability of mammals, including humans, to re-grow new hair cells instead of damaged ones. Therefore, external devices like hearing instruments or implants are needed. Hearing instruments amplify and modulate sound frequencies, where hearing ability is not completely lost. They convert sound frequencies of completely damaged hair cells to sound frequencies of still functional hair cells. On the other hand, cochlear implants generate electric signals in cochlear with the help of an electrode inserted into it, and thus completely replace the hearing function of hair cells with the electrode.

A small number of people may have a mixed hearing loss, where a part of the hearing loss is due to the conductive hearing loss, and another part is due to the sensorineural hearing loss.

2.3 Cultural Perspective on Hearing Disability

International Classification[11] of Impairments, Disabilities, and Handicaps defines "hearing loss" as a combination of "hearing impairment", "hearing disability", and "hearing handicap". Hearing impairment is the dysfunction of the hearing sense measurable in the laboratory or clinic. Hearing disability is the auditory difficulty experienced by an individual in daily life. Hearing handicap is the non-auditory effect of hearing disability on daily life. Later Stephens and Kerr (2000) proposed to replace the terms "impairment", "disability", and "handicap" with "function", "activity", and "participation" in order to include not only negative, but also positive consequences of a specific health status. This research focuses on negative aspects of hearing loss compared with normal hearing. Therefore, the terms "impairment", "disability", and "handicap" are used as described in International Classification of Impairments, Disabilities, and Handicaps.

There are many ways of understanding and interpreting hearing disability from cultural perspective. The three main models of understanding hearing disability[12] are the following:

- The medical model defines hearing disability as an individual hearing health problem, illness or impairment. The focus is on the hearing impaired. The main question answered in this model is, what kind of a treatment and rehabilitation process is to apply to a specific person with a specific hearing loss to get the best possible result. The majority of hearing impaired people acquire the disability in adult life. These people still remember how it used to be when they were able to hear normally. For them hearing loss is a sensory deficit in their body. They report difficulties in following conversations, issues in social participation, and struggle to stay alert in noisy surroundings.
- The social model defines disability as a limitation imposed by social, cultural and economic barriers on full participation in social life. People who are born severely hearing impaired or profoundly deaf, and were not fitted with a hearing instrument or an implant within several months after birth, learn to communicate with sign language. They often join the deaf community, which defines their social experience. These people do not have past experience of normal hearing. Therefore, the limited social participation and interactions, rather than a burdensome disease, are relevant for the social model.
- Under the human rights model, disability is the result of equal opportunities limitations imposed by social, cultural, and environmental barriers on individuals with medical conditions. The main problem addressed in the human

11 World Health Organization, 1980.
12 Handicap International, 2006.

rights model is the discrimination and exclusion of the hearing impaired. At the same time, the importance of medical intervention is recognized. The main goal of this model is to empower the hearing impaired and guarantee their rights and active participation in political, economic, social, and cultural life to be equal to those without hearing loss.

For any model of understanding the hearing impairment from the cultural perspective described above, hearing loss leads to personal, social, and economic consequences. This research looks at minimizing these costs with the help of a better healthcare economic policy for hearing impairment.

2.4 Economic Situation of the Hearing Impaired

"Hearing impairment is the most frequent sensory deficit in human populations, affecting more than 250 million people in the world" [13]. People with untreated hearing loss are highly over-represented among the poor in the developing world. Current research[14] stresses that there is a strong correlation between poverty and illness. Poverty is considered both the cause and the consequence of untreated hearing loss. Poverty is the cause of hearing loss since poor often lack resources to protect themselves against diseases. They typically live in an environment with higher noise pollution. Due to the nature of their daily activities, they are more prone to receive injuries or diseases, some of which may lead to hearing loss. A population with insufficient economic resources is not able to provide for sufficient health care.[15] Therefore, a society with low income has a tendency to have poorer health. On the other hand, poverty is the consequence of the untreated hearing loss, since the hearing impaired often lack access to education, health services, and many income-generating activities, especially those activities which require the ability to understand speech and sounds from the surrounding environment. This can be illustrated with the help of Figure 8.

Kochkin (2007) shows that even in such a high-income country like the US the price of hearing aids is a major obstacle for adoption of these devices (Figure 9). His study shows that "Three out of four (76%) respondents mentioned financial constraints as a barrier to hearing aid adoption".[16] Besides,

13 Mathers et al., 2003, p. 1.

14 World Health Organization, 2001, Suhrcke et al., 2005.

15 Moeller et al., 2004.

16 Kochkin, 2007, p. 37.

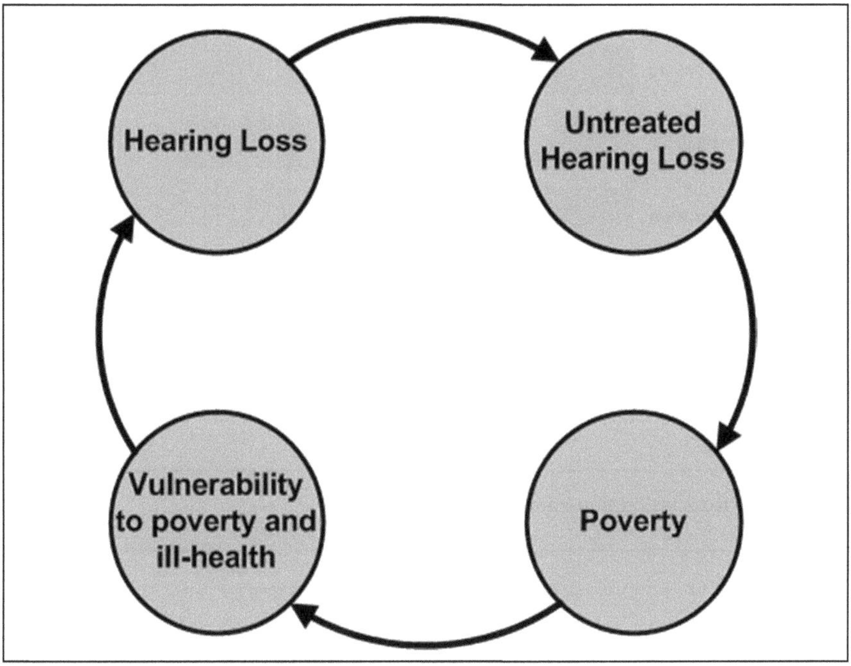

Figure 8: The vicious circle between poverty and hearing loss.[17]

"64% indicated they cannot afford hearing aids, while nearly half (49%) indicated it is a definite reason why they don't use hearing aids"[18].

Kochkin (2007) quantifies the income gap between those, who can afford hearing aids, and those, who cannot. The Figure 10 shows this income gap for different age groups.

> "Three of the five age groups show close to a $40,000 differential in income, while in the youngest segment (age 21-44) we find a $30,000 differential and in the elderly segment (75+) an income differential of $21,000." [19]

This finding underlines the importance of hearing aids affordability as a major pre-requisite for wider adoption of hearing aids both in developed and in developing countries.

---

[17] Own illustration following Handicap International (2006), p. 16.

[18] Kochkin, 2007, p. 37.

[19] Kochkin, 2007, p. 38.

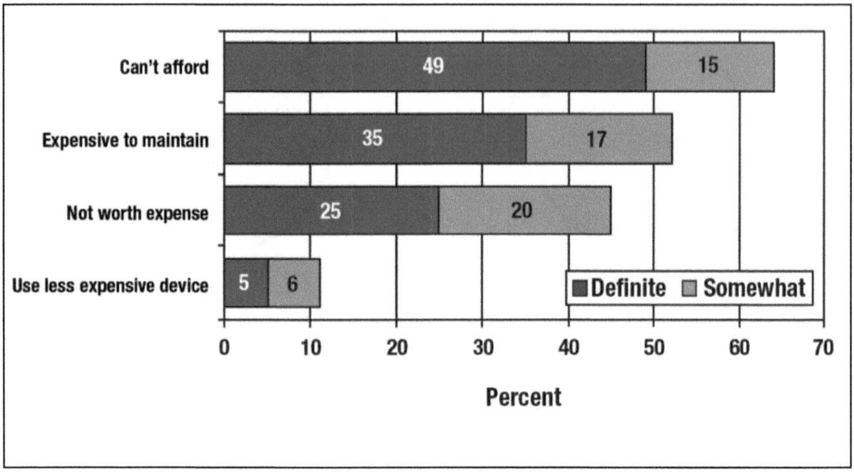

Figure 9: Reasons for non-adoption of hearing aids.[20]

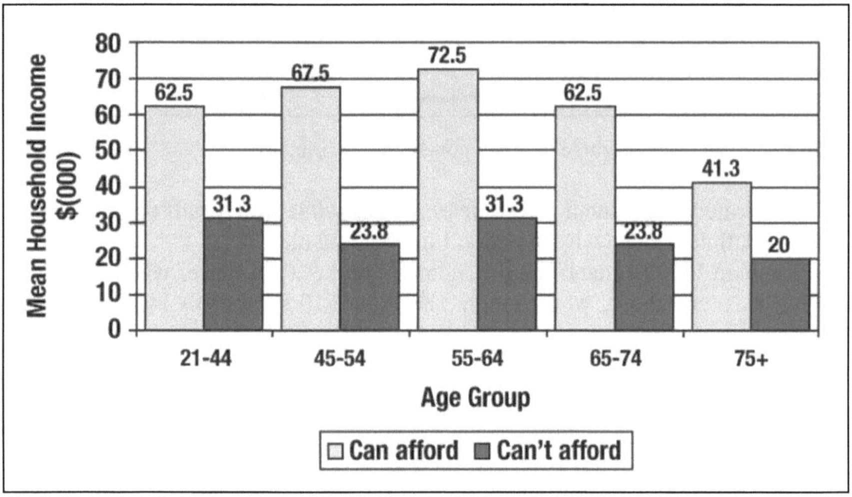

Figure 10: Median income comparing people who state they can and cannot afford hearing aids controlling for age.[21]

[20] Kochkin, 2007, p. 34, fig. 4c.

[21] Kochkin, 2007, p. 34, fig. 5.

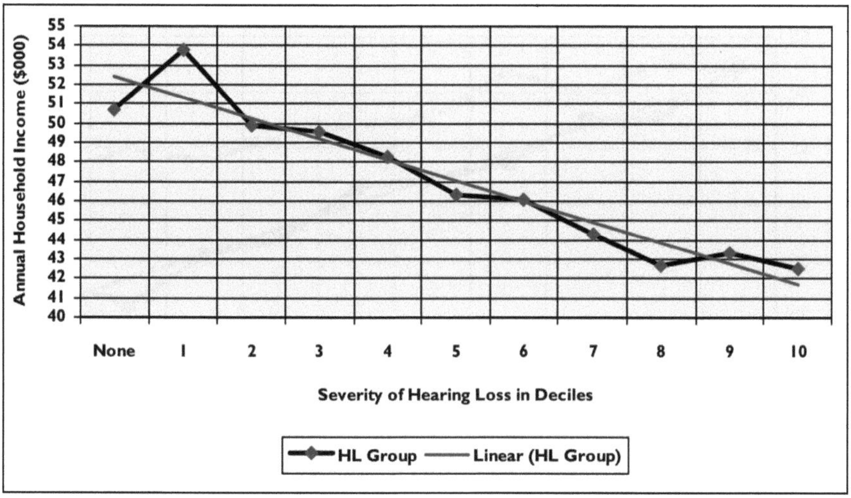

Figure 11: Relationship between hearing loss and household income.[22]

Figure 11 shows that the income level of the hearing impaired (both aided and unaided) negatively correlates with the severity of their hearing loss degree.

> "Individuals with the most serious hearing loss (decile 10) could be expected to earn $12,000 less per year than an individual with a mild (decile 1) hearing loss."[23]

Kochkin (2005) investigates what are the real economic benefits of wearing hearing instruments.

> "While both treated and untreated hearing loss groups show deterioration of income as their hearing loss worsens, the income decline is cut in half for hearing aid owners."[24]

Figure 12 shows that aided hearing helps to slow down the income decline with the increase of hearing loss.

> "... we found no evidence of an association between hearing loss and unemployment for any age group. An unexplained finding is that aided subjects tended to be employed more often than normal-hearing subjects and than unaided subjects, though the relationships were insignificant."[25]

---

[22] Kochkin, 2005, p. 6, fig. 1.
[23] Kochkin, 2005, p. 6.
[24] Kochkin, 2005, p. 7.
[25] Kochkin, 2010, pp. 23.

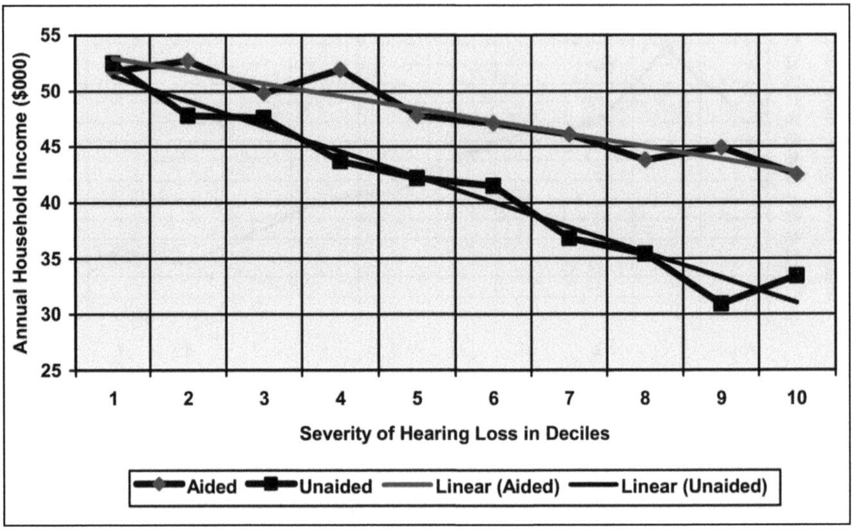

Figure 12: Relationship between hearing loss and household income comparing aided and unaided people.[26]

More specifically,

> "There is no significant relationship between hearing loss and unemployment rates for aided subjects (p<0.07). However, there is a significant relationship between unaided subjects and unemployment (p<0.0003), with unemployment rates increasing significantly as a function of hearing loss."[27]

The unemployment rate for aided and unaided hearing impaired for different levels of hearing loss is shown in the Figure 13.

In his study, Ruben (2001) shows that income of the hearing impaired is 40% to 45% lower than that of the people without hearing impairment. The unemployment rate among the hearing impaired is up to 20% higher than that of a normal hearing population. In addition, low income is more common among the hearing impaired.[28] More specifically, depending on the degree of hearing loss, up to 43.7% of the hearing impaired are in a low-income group, while for people with no severe disabilities this number only reaches 19.3%.

[26] Kochkin, 2005, p. 7, fig. 2.
[27] Kochkin, 2010, pp. 23-24.
[28] Ruben, 2001.

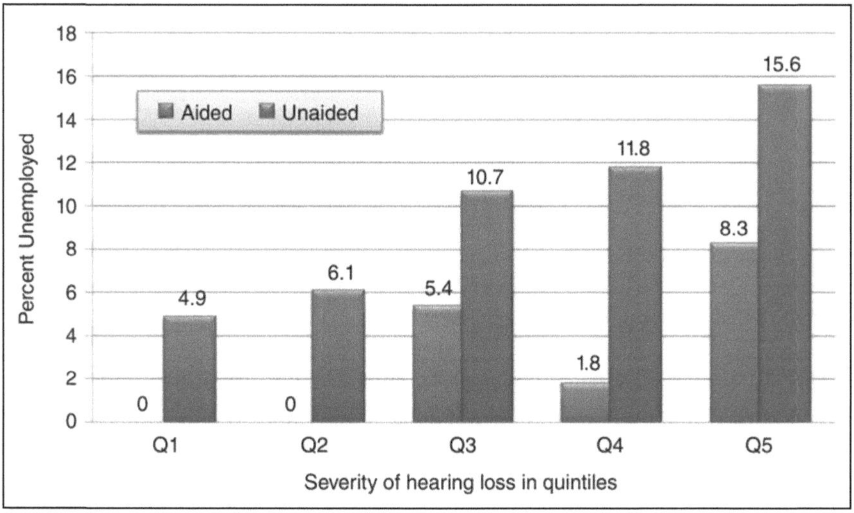

Figure 13: Unemployment rates by hearing loss quintile comparing aided and unaided subjects.[29]

The increasing utilization of communication skills in jobs of the 21st century also means that increasingly more people with unaided hearing loss will be unemployed. Hearing is critical to effective communication in the workplace. Not only many employers require proficiency in spoken communication, but also in some cases, hearing is vital to assure safety on the job. Unaided hearing impaired have a higher risk of making mistakes at work, have higher rates of unemployment, and experience overall reduced quality of life.

> "Like the rest of the population in developing economies, most people with disabilities turn to self-employment because of a lack of opportunities in the job market. Although many would prefer to have a job with a regular income, self-employment is often the only option available. It is estimated that for each person with disability employed by a company in developing countries, four more generate their own income through self-employment, most of them in the informal sector. In contrast, in developed countries, less than three per cent of people with disabilities are self-employed."[30]

29 Kochkin, 2010, p. 24, fig. 5.
30 Handicap International, 2006, p. 17.

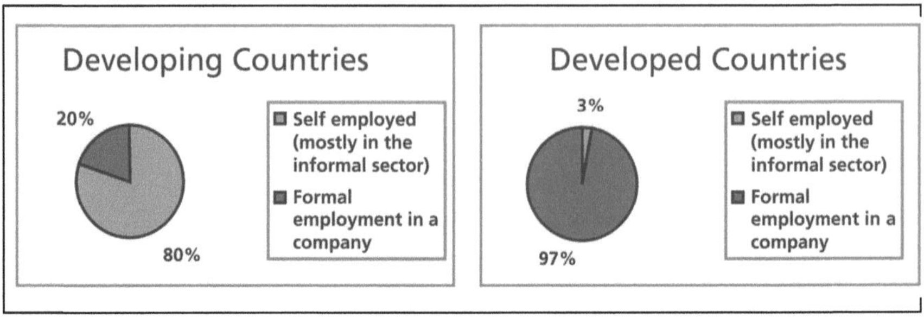

Figure 14: Comparison of self-employment for people with disabilities.[31]

Figure 14 compares self-employment for people with disabilities in developed and developing countries. In the developing economies

> "Many people with disabilities have started shops, craft workshops and farming activities; others are involved in street vending, tailoring, carpentry, etc."[32]

2.5 Cost of Hearing Impairment

Mathers et al. (2003) uses the years lived with disability (YLD) as a measure of burden of a specific disability.

> "Total global YLD for hearing loss are estimated to be 24.9 million or 4.7% of total YLD due to all causes. This makes hearing loss the second leading cause of YLD after depression, and gives it a larger non-fatal burden than alcohol use disorders, osteoarthritis and schizophrenia"[33]

Not all hearing impaired equally suffer from hearing loss. The need for aided hearing may vary depending on the degree and type of hearing loss. Since hearing loss places limitations on daily activities of the hearing impaired and on their employment opportunities, it is important to be able to measure the burden of hearing loss. The measurements help to identify the degree of the hearing impaireds' exclusion from society. Knowing the degree of the exclusion from society for each individual hearing impaired person, it is possible to make a better decision on allocation of the scarce health resources such as reimbursements or subsidies for purchase of hearing aids. Economic evaluations are used to help making the decision on the allocation of the health resources.

[31] Handicap International, (2006), p. 17, fig. 2.
[32] Handicap International, 2006, p. 17.
[33] Mathers et al., 2003, p. 23.

> "Economic evaluations typically involve making comparisons between two or more options (one option could include doing nothing – i.e. no treatment)." [34]

> "Three main types of economic evaluation are used for health care interventions: cost-benefit analysis, cost-effectiveness analysis, and cost-utility analysis." [35]

> "Cost-benefit analysis involves comparing the monetary benefits of an intervention to its costs. If the monetary benefits exceed the costs, then the intervention may be considered as worthwhile. A limitation of cost-benefit analysis is the difficulty in assigning money values to improvements in health status or extensions to length of life." [36]

> "A more common method of economic evaluation is cost-effectiveness analysis, where the costs of an intervention are related to some health outcome, such as lives saved or cases detected." [37]

> "Cost-utility analysis is used to determine the effect of a health care intervention on both quality and length of life, which are then combined into a single summary measure such as a quality adjusted life year (QALY)." [38]

> "Cost-utility analysis has the advantage over cost-effectiveness analysis in that it can be used to compare across programmes with different health outcomes." [39]

Cost-utility analysis is particularly useful for treatments that do not impact survival or longevity, but have the direct impact on quality of life. This is exactly the case with hearing loss.

In Cost-utility analysis, the cost is measured in monetary units. Utility is calculated in quality-adjusted life years (QALY). "The QALY is a composite measure that combines information on both the length and quality of life."[40] A year lived in perfect health is assigned the value of 1. Death is assigned the value of 0. A year lived with unaided hearing loss has a value between 0 and 1. A year lived with aided hearing loss also has a value between 0 and 1, but it is higher than a value of a year lived with unaided hearing loss.

In case of hearing impairment, the cost associated with fitting a hearing instrument includes the expenses on hearing screening, the hearing instrument, fitting the hearing instrument to match the hearing loss, rehabilitation, and maintenance of the hearing instrument. For a hearing implant the costs include the money on diagnosis, surgery, implant with the sound processor, rehabilita-

---

34 Williams et al., 2012, p. 50.
35 Clarke et al., 2013, p. 82.
36 Clarke et al., 2013, p. 82.
37 Clarke et al., 2013, p. 82.
38 Clarke et al., 2013, p. 82.
39 Clarke et al., 2013, p. 82.
40 Williams et al., 2012, p. 51.

tion, and maintenance of the implant system. In both cases, utility is measured in QALY. It reflects changes in physical function, mental health, bodily discomfort and ability to lead normal social life of a hearing impaired person compared to a person with normal hearing.

Through the years, multiple studies were performed to determine the Cost-utility of hearing aids. The most notable ones were done by Cheng and Niparko (1999), Wong et al. (2000), Niparko (2009), Ruben (2001), Joore et al. (2003), Keren at al. (2002), and Mohr et al. (2000). The results of all these studies are quite consistent. Cheng and Niparko (1999) identified the health utility of profoundly deaf adults to be 0.54 QALY. This means that the average loss of health utility as a result of profound deafness is 0.46=1-0.54 QALY. The average gain in health utility after the implantation was 0.26 QALY, resulting in health utility value of 0.8 QALY (=1-0.54+0.26) with cochlear implants. Summerfield et al. (2002) found health utility loss to be at 0.44 QALY (=1-0.56) prior to cochlear implantation for profoundly deaf. Joore et al. (2003) analyzed the situation of 80 hearing impaired with moderate hearing loss. Their finding was that hearing loss leads to health utility loss of 0.48 QALY, resulting in health utility value of 0.52 QALY. After fitting with hearing aids the health utility gain was 0.26 QALY, causing health utility growth up to 0.78 QALY.

2.6 Hearing Loss and Comorbidities: Psychological Effects of Hearing Loss

Hearing loss affects a person's cognitive functioning as well as quality of life. Lin et al. (2011) at John Hopkins University in colaboration with the National Institute of Aging performed a study of seniors with hearing loss using data collected during Baltimore Longitudial Study on Aging. The study investigated the connection between hearing loss and dimentia in 639 individuals. Out of 639 participants 184 individuals had hearing loss, while 455 individuals had no hearing loss at the time of enrollment. Of those, who had hearing loss, 125 had mild hearing loss, 53 had moderate hearing loss, and 6 had severe hearing loss. None of the participants showed any signs of dimentia at the time of enrollment in the study between 1990 and 1994. Almost 12 years after the enrollment, 58 cases of dimentia were diagnosed. Of them, 20 cases (4.4% of the group's population) were in the normal hearing group, 21 case (16.8% of the group's population) – in the mild hearing loss group, 15 cases (28.3% of the group's population) – in the moderate hearing loss group, and 2 cases (33.3% of the group's population) – in the severe hearing loss. The study found a stisticially significant correlation between having a hearing loss at the time of enrollement, and having dimentia disease 12 years later.

Wilson et al. (1992) point out to underestimation of comorbidities associated with hearing loss. They identified such comordibities of hearing loss as hypertension and diabetes. The Blue Mountains Hearing Study[41] also reported that older people with hearing loss (>25 dB) were more likely to report diabetes, as well as a history of stroke. Hogan et al. (2001) identified heart attack and psychiatric disorders to be associated with self-reported poor hearing.

2.7 Hearing Prosthesis Devices

Many types of hearing loss cannot be reversed. Both hearing instruments and implants used to treat hearing loss are hearing prosthesis devices. Though they cannot reverse hearing loss, people with hearing disability can restore their ability to listen and communicate successfully with the help of hearing instruments or implants. Hearing aids not only improve social and emotional well-being, but also they often increase chances for better employment in the future. In this section, we give an overview of various hearing prosthesis devices.

First, we examine different types of hearing instruments. Then, an overview of hearing implants is given.

The main principles of how a hearing instrument works are the following. First, sound comes in via microphones. Then it is processed inside an analog or digital signal processing chip in order to determine which part of the incoming sound needs to be suppressed, which one needs to be amplified, and which part needs to be shifted or compressed to other frequencies. After processing, the sound is reproduced via a loudspeaker, called a receiver, into a patients' ear.

There are different types of hearing instruments:

- Sound amplifiers or assistive listening devices
- Pocket hearing aids
- Behind-the-ear (BTE), Over-the-ear (OTE), and Receiver-in-the-ear (RITE) hearing aids
- Custom hearing aids
- CROS/BiCROS solutions

The simplest kind of hearing devices is a sound amplifier or an assistive listening device. It comes in all kinds of forms and shapes, most often as pocket hearing aids, behind-the-ear hearing aids, or a one-size-fits-all in-the-ear instrument. Such devices are widely available and relatively cheaply priced (USD 22-26 per

41 Mitchell, 2002.

device). The principle of working of a sound amplifier is to amplify all incoming sounds almost at the same rate. It does not require an audiologist to fine-tune it, since it does not have the sophistication of different amplification at different frequencies. As discussed above, sensorineural hearing loss typically requires different amplification at different frequencies, therefore self-fitting patients with such assistive listening devices will often cause negative experience, which might, in turn, lead to lower willingness to try more sophisticated hearing instruments. Nevertheless, in some cases, especially when there is relatively equal hearing loss at different frequencies, such devices can help patients to hear better. Most often, such a profile of hearing loss occurs in case of conductive hearing loss. Although sound amplifiers are helpful here, it is important to keep in mind that many cases of conductive hearing loss can be reversed, and therefore do not require hearing aids.

Pocket hearing aids are one of the oldest hearing instrument forms. Current pocket hearing aids have the same sound processing technology like behind-the-ear hearing instruments – analog or digital, although they tend to be at the lower level of technology. The main advantage of pocket hearing aids compared to behind-the-ear or in-the-ear instruments, is that they use bigger batteries (typically AA) and have larger controls. The former is attractive for very low-income consumers, who are reluctant to get a behind-the-ear hearing instrument due to the cost of batteries; AA batteries are cheaper and much more widely available. They are attractive for older people with severe dexterity issues. Another advantage of pocket hearing aids is that the microphone is located on the hearing aid, and it is possible to give the hearing aid to the speaker if she/he stands next to the hearing impaired. This leads to better speech understanding, especially in noisy environments. The disadvantage of the pocket hearing aids is that they are big, require corded headphones and are not convenient to use in many practical situations. Since there is no price advantage of pocket hearing aids compared to behind-the-ear hearing aids with analog or trimmer digital technology, many consumers in the developing countries prefer to use behind-the-ear instruments, as they allow for much more flexibility in daily activities.

Trimmer and analog hearing aids work well only in case of linear hearing loss. Sensorineural hearing loss is generally downward sloping with less hearing loss at lower frequencies, and higher hearing loss at higher frequencies. People often have a unique profile of downward sloping hearing loss. Trimmer, and analog devices do not work well in such situations. Besides, since advanced digital sound processing features are not available in these devices, the performance of such hearing instruments in noisy environments, in cars, in restaurants and other locations is quite poor. Trimmer and analog devices can show an acceptable performance only in one-to-one conversations in quiet environment for customers with linear hearing loss.

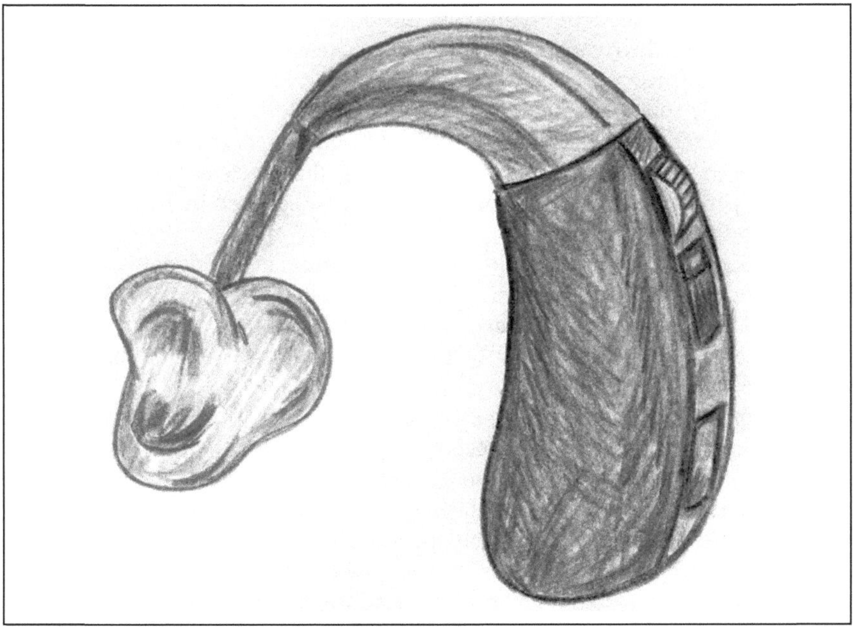

Figure 15: BTE with an earmold.

The most commonly used type of hearing aid is behind-the-ear (BTE). It is shown in Figure 15.

A behind-the-ear instrument is often equipped with a directional microphone system. It allows amplifying sounds coming towards the front of a hearing instrument user, downplaying the noise that comes from the sides or behind. Microphones are usually covered with windscreens in order to protect them from wind noise, dirt and humidity. In classical BTE instruments, a receiver is located in the body of the instrument. The amplified sound flows from the receiver via ear hook, tube and individually manufactured earmold into the outer ear of a patient.

A battery compartment is usually located at the bottom of a behind-the-ear instrument. This location of a battery is typical for BTE hearing instruments, mainly because it allows the center of mass of a hearing instrument to be moved down, which ensures the secure position of a hearing instrument behind the ear.

As a rule, behind-the-ear hearing instruments can be switched on and off by a user. It is also possible to change hearing programs and/or volume without qualified help. Some of these functions can be easily accessed via control elements on a hearing instrument, while others can be used via a remote control. The prerequisite for a remote control to work with a hearing instrument is the availability of two induction coils, one inside the hearing instrument and the second one inside the remote. This enables exchange of wireless signals between the two mechanisms.

The whole sound-conduction system of a behind-the-ear hearing instrument including the ear hook, the tube, the earmold (along with a ventilation channel and resonance space), and residual volume inside the ear canal is important. The acoustical performance of the whole system can be adjusted by modifying parts of the sound conduction system.[42]

Besides, depth of an earmold, and with it associated residual space in the ear canal, can change the amplification of a hearing instrument. For example, two times decrease of residual space in the canal theoretically leads to the amplification increase of 6 dB. Practically this value is a little bit smaller, because the ear canal is not a sound-proof cavity.[43]

Depending on the shape of an ear canal, power level of a hearing instrument and hearing loss, it is sometimes recommended to create a funnel-shaped sound channel in the earmold. Such form of a sound channel is especially important for reproduction of sounds in high frequency area of 3000 Hz and more. Just by using a different sound channel shape, it is possible to reach an additional amplification of 10-15 dB. This effect is achieved by creating a resonance effect in a sound channel of an earmold for specific sound wave frequencies.

Another important part of behind-the-ear hearing instrument acoustics is a ventilation channel in the earmold. It is typically located parallel to a sound channel. A ventilation channel function is to allow a low frequency part of sound to leave the ear canal, at the same time keeping high frequency sound inside. The size of a ventilation channel makes it impossible for high frequency sounds to escape. This enables decrease of hearing instrument power in the area below 1000 Hz.

As was mentioned above, sensorineural hearing loss is commonly downward sloping from low to high frequencies. Thus, in the area of low frequencies less amplification is needed. This reduction in low frequency amplification happens partially due to a ventilation channel. In addition, a ventilation channel provides ventilation for the residual space in the ear canal in order to reduce the air pressure on the ear drum. Besides, it also helps to reduce the occlusion effect, which happens to be one of the primary reasons for the hearing impaired to refuse using hearing instruments. It occurs when the ear canal is closed. In such cases, a person hears hollow sounds of her/his own voice. You can simulate the effect by closing your own ears firmly with two fingers and speaking loud.

---

[42] Voogdt, 2005.

[43] Voogdt, 2005.

The reason behind the occlusion effect is the following. There are two ways for the sound of voice to reach the ear drum. One way is external via air and the outer ear. Another one is internal through the Eustachian tube in the inner ear. When there is no hearing instrument in the ear, the excess sound pressure delivered via the human body leaves the ear through the ear canal. When the ear canal is closed with a hearing aid completely, the own voice sound transferred via the human body stays inside. This produces an unnatural hollow sound of one's own voice and is often described as "speaking in a barrel". If a hearing instrument allows for sufficient air circulation in the outer ear, the occlusion effect can be significantly reduced up to a level where a patient perceives her/his own voice as natural. Acoustically the occlusion effect is dependent on the size of a ventilation channel. The degree of the perceived occlusion effect is directly proportional to the vent length and reversely proportional to the square of vent diameter. The occlusion reduction due to big venting channels is highly correlated with acceptance of hearing aids by patients.

As a side note, it is worth mentioning that there are also disadvantages when using big vents. One of them is audio feedback. It appears when a sound signal travels in a continuous loop between an audio input and an audio output. The result is a screeching noise, which occurs when sound that comes out of a hearing instrument leaves an ear canal via a venting channel and then gets picked up again by hearing instrument microphones. Vent size increase leads to acoustic leakage increase, which in turn increases the probability of feedback. Audio feedback takes place only above a certain level of sound amplification in case of open fitting, namely fitting with instruments with relatively big venting channels.

Another major disadvantage of using big vents is a sound delay effect. It occurs due to a time difference between the moment sound comes in through a vent naturally, and the moment the same sound comes out of a hearing instrument after sound processing. It results in an echo or barrel effect when a patient speaks.

Technological advances in the past few years have partially solved these issues in digital hearing instruments. In modern digital hearing instruments, digital sound-processing has reached very high speed. The time delay difference between sound processed in a hearing instrument and sound that comes in via a vent has become extremely small (less than 5 ms). Nowadays patients fitted with modern digital hearing aids no longer perceive the time delay as unpleasant. Besides that, feedback cancellation technologies in digital hearing aids allow for about 15-20 dB higher amplification in hearing instruments with big vents than it was possible before. These developments significantly increase the target audience for open fitting.

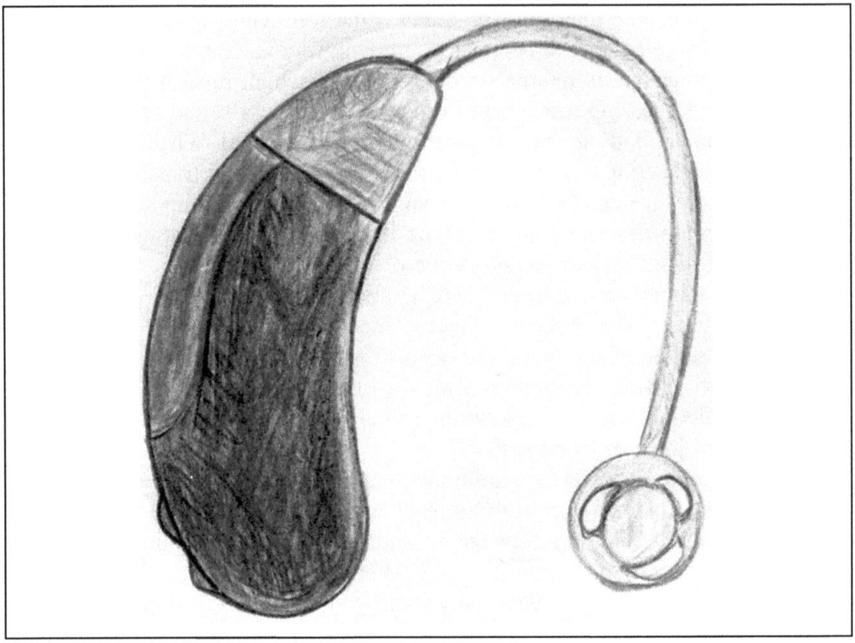

Figure 16: Over-the-ear (OTE) hearing instrument.

As a result, two additional sub-types of behind-the-ear devices have been developed and has become available on the market in the past years:

- Over-the-ear (OTE) devices with a thin tube that is smaller than 1 mm in diameter, and open silicone dome in the ear canal, instead of a custom-made earmold
- Receiver-in-the-ear (RITE) devices, where a receiver (a loudspeaker) is located directly in the ear canal

The main advantage[44] of an over-the-ear device with open silicone dome (Figure 16) is that the occlusion effect is so small that it is practically nonexistent. In addition, comparing to standard behind-the-ear devices, over-the-ear hearing aids are smaller, have no ear hook, but have a very thin tube, which makes them less visible to an observer. Besides open silicone domes, closed tulip-shaped domes are offered. They allow for higher amplification, but still give less occlusion effect than normal earmolds do.

44 Kiessling et al., (2005).

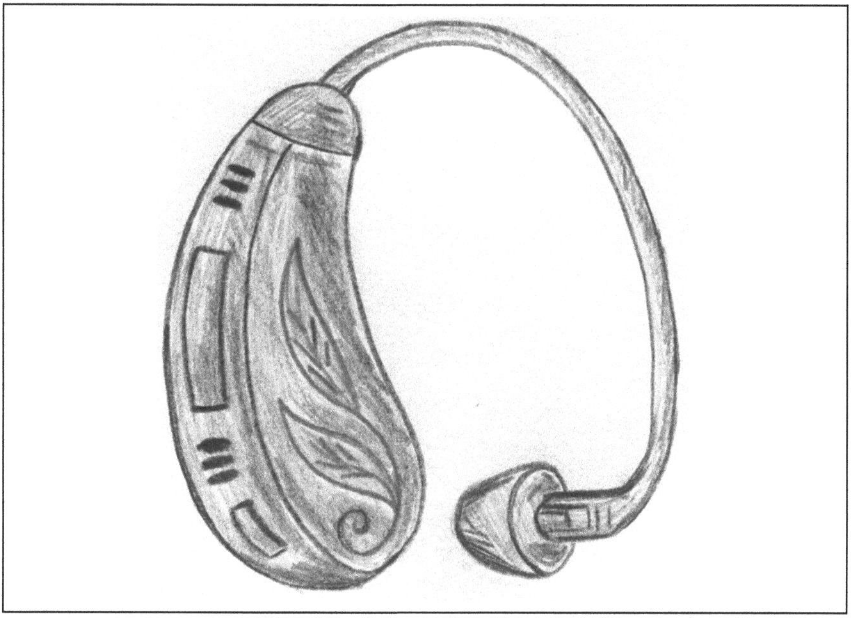

Figure 17: Receiver-in-the-ear (RITE) hearing instrument.

Receiver-in-the-ear (RITE) devices (Figure 17) are small and cosmetically attractive due to receiver location in the ear canal. Similar to over-the-ear hearing aids, RITE hearing aids are also well equipped to offer open fitting. However, unlike an extremely thin over-the-ear device tube, a RITE device receiver leaves the canal less open.

Receiver-in-the-ear hearing aids are available with open or closed dome. If needed, an earmold can be produced for higher amplification instruments. A RITE device's receiver is easily replaced if damaged by ear wax. Over-the-ear and receiver-in-the-ear devices are used in situations when open fitting is requested.

Custom hearing instruments are typically offered in 3 sizes: full-concha or in-the-ear (ITE), in-the-canal (ITC) and completely-in-the-canal (CIC). The examples are shown in Figure 18, Figure 19 and Figure 20. Similar to earmolds, they are custom-made for each individual ear. Manufacturing of a custom hearing instrument is much more complex than of an earmold. The reason behind it is that the whole instrument, including a microphone(s), an amplifier, a receiver, a venting channel etc., has to be located in the pinna and/or canal area. Nothing is placed behind the ear.

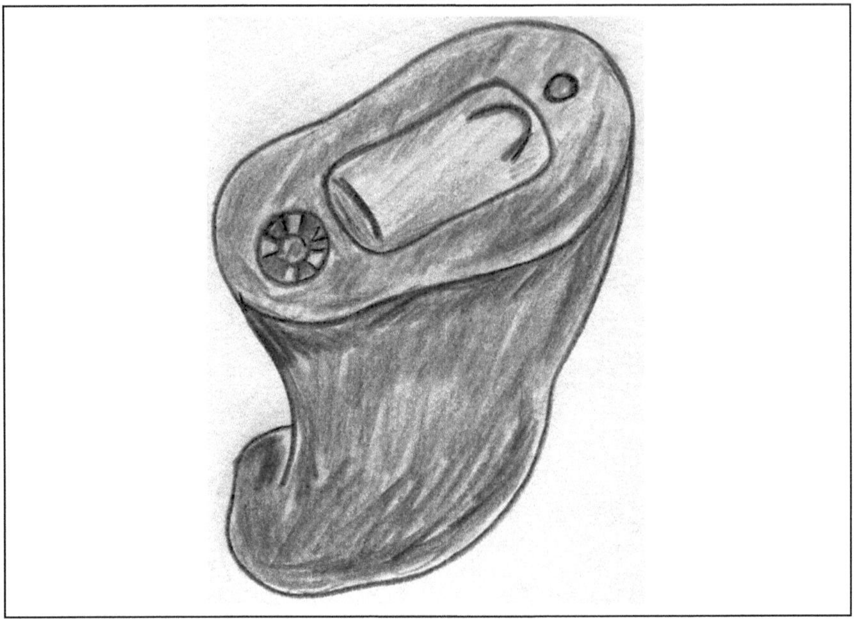

Figure 18: In-the-ear (ITE) custom hearing instrument.

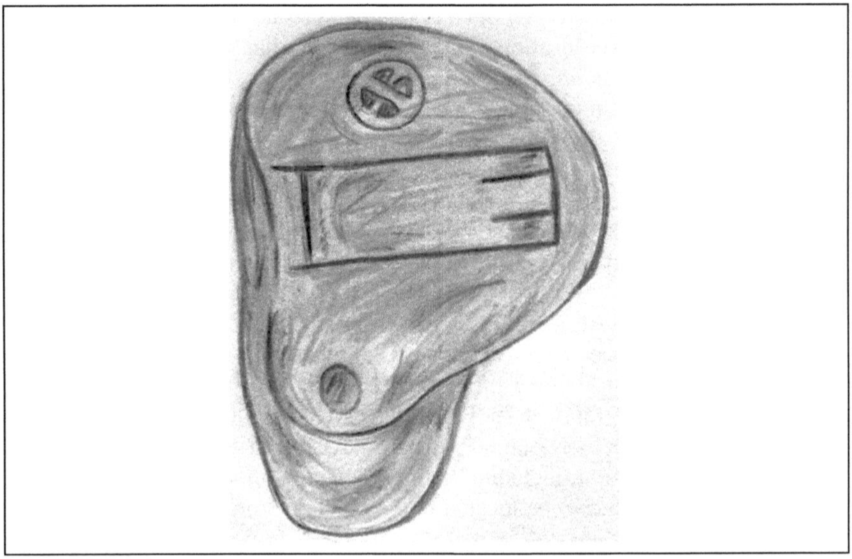

Figure 19: In-the-canal (ITC) custom hearing instrument.

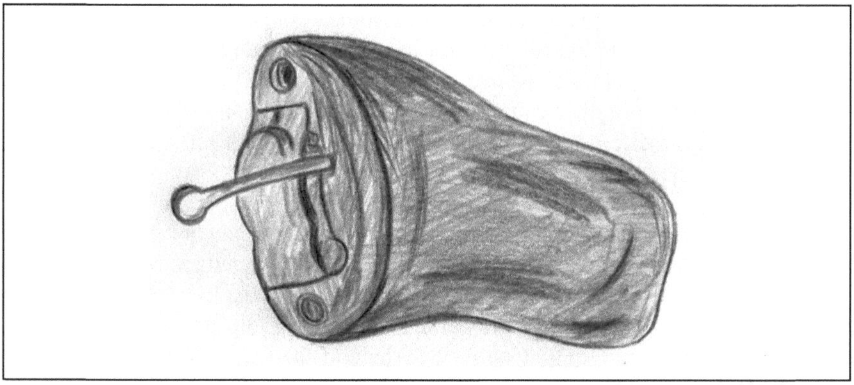

Figure 20: Completely-in-canal (CIC) custom hearing instrument.

Lately, many manufacturers started offering Invisible-in-the-canal (IIC) devices (Figure 21) that are built even smaller than completely-in-canal, but are still based on 10A-size battery.

Figure 21: Invisible-in-canal (IIC) hearing instrument.

If there is enough free space in the ear, some control elements like Program Switch, and/or Volume Control are built in a custom-made hearing aid. Unfortunately, especially for smaller device sizes, space availability is limited. In such cases hearing aids are either equipped with induction coil in order to allow for a remote control, or offered without the possibility to switch programs or change volume (all IIC devices and some CIC devices).

Custom hearing aids are produced individually for a specific ear canal of a patient. The fitting process for them is more complex than for behind-the-ear devices. As behind-the-ear hearing aids are serially manufactured in hearing instrument factories, a hearing aid dispenser has a BTE device almost always at hand. She/he can take it out of a drawer and start fitting immediately after having taken a patient's audiogram. Contrary to behind-the-ear hearing aids, custom instruments have to be custom-made first.

Non-custom-made in-the-ear hearing aids also exist. Unfortunately, they have a lot of issues, as every individual has a unique shape of the ear canal. First, the sit of a hearing instrument in the ear is not comfortable. Second, undefined sit results in ventilation not only through the venting channel, but also through the sides of an instrument improperly sitting in the ear, causing feedback at much lower gain, than the one that can be achieved with a custom-made instrument. All these are the main reasons behind the low popularity of instant-fit in-the-ear devices.

Before the actual audiological fitting of a custom device to the patient's hearing loss, a custom hearing aid has to be manufactured to physically fit the ear of the patient. Most of the custom hearing instruments are produced with additive manufacturing technology called stereolithography.[45]

The acoustic advantage of in-the-ear custom devices is the microphone positioning in the ear canal. Due to sound reception in the ear, the natural pinna effect allows directional sound reception, even if only one microphone is provided. In custom hearing instruments, a receiver is also located in the ear canal. This makes it possible to use a very short sound tube (less than 10 mm) with the resonance above 10 kHz, so that no disturbing resonance effects take place in the sound transmission area. Cosmetically small custom hearing devices (CIC and IIC) are also attractive to the users, because they allow the hearing impaired hide the fact that hearing aids are being used.

The main disadvantage of custom hearing instruments, similarly to receiver-in-the-ear devices, is the impossibility of completely open fitting, as hearing instrument components take up too much space in the ear canal. Using wide and short venting channels in custom hearing instruments can marginally decrease

45 Voogdt, 2005.

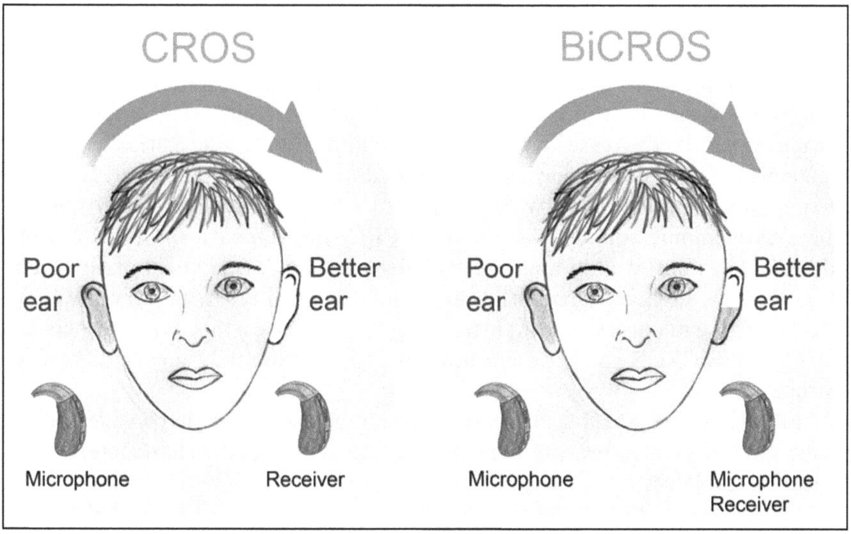

Figure 22: CROS/BiCROS solutions.

the occlusion effect.[46] Nevertheless, over-the-ear hearing instruments currently offer the best occlusion reduction. Another disadvantage of custom hearing instruments is their high cost comparing to BTE devices.

In cases of profound deafness or extremely severe hearing loss in one of the ears, CROS/BiCROS solutions (Figure 22) are considered. Usually, in such situations a microphone is placed on the deaf side. Then the sound from the microphone is transmitted to the functioning ear. One way to implement CROS/BiCROS systems is a connection of two behind-the-ear units either by wire or by wireless transmission. Another way is to incorporate such a system into eyeglasses.

A CROS (Contralateral Routing of Signal) system, where on one side is a microphone, and on the other side a receiver, makes it possible to achieve feedback-free open fitting. This is due to the natural separation that happens between a receiver and a microphone, since both are located on opposite sides of the patient's head. Responsiveness on the deaf side is increased as well. Unfortunately, natural space recognition of sounds and selective hearing is not possible. In the CROS case, hearing remains monaural. Due to reduced directionality, it is unrealistic to expect substantial benefit with a CROS device in noisy environment,

46 Jespersen et al, 2006.

but in one-to-one conversations the performance is good. The acceptance of CROS hearing aids is low.[47]

A BiCROS (Bilateral Contralateral Routing of Signal) solution is often recommended when one ear is profoundly deaf and the other one has moderate hearing loss.[48] In this case, both ears are equipped with microphones, and the signals from both microphones are transmitted into the functioning ear. BiCROS hearing aids are much more widespread than CROS.[49] Given that only one ear processes incoming sounds, same as with CROS instruments, BiCROS hearing aids do not perform well in noisy environment. As the development of new technology allows higher degrees of hearing loss to be fitted with very powerful hearing aids without feedback, increasingly more cases that were previously suitable for BiCROS solutions are now fitted with extremely powerful hearing instruments.

In cases where hearing instruments cannot be used, more expensive and invasive solutions called hearing implants are considered. There are different types of hearing implants:

- Bone anchored hearing aid (BAHA)
- Middle-ear implants
- Cochlear implants
- Auditory Brain Implants

When a patient has conductive hearing loss and surgery is not possible or has repeatedly led to negative outcomes, bone anchored hearing aids (BAHA) or middle ear implants (Figure 23 and 24) can be considered.

BAHA solutions are especially effective for patients with chronic otitis media, middle or outer ear malformations.[50] A BAHA system consists of a surgically implanted titanium prosthesis, which is embedded into the skull of a patient, and a sound processor. The sound processor consists of a microphone, an amplifier, a vibrator that generates bone vibrations, and a battery. In order to achieve the required efficiency of the sound processor, it should be able to generate strong vibration signals. For this reason, a BAHA sound processor has a certain minimum weight. This requirement on the minimum weight negatively affects the cosmetics of such hearing aids. Besides, building an extremely small BAHA device is not possible due to physical limitations on density of materials used in producing it.

47 Kiessling et al, 2008.
48 Del Dot, Hickson, and O'Connel, 1992.
49 Kiessling et al, 2008.
50 Hakansson et al., 1985; Tjellström et al., 2001; Snik et al., 2005.

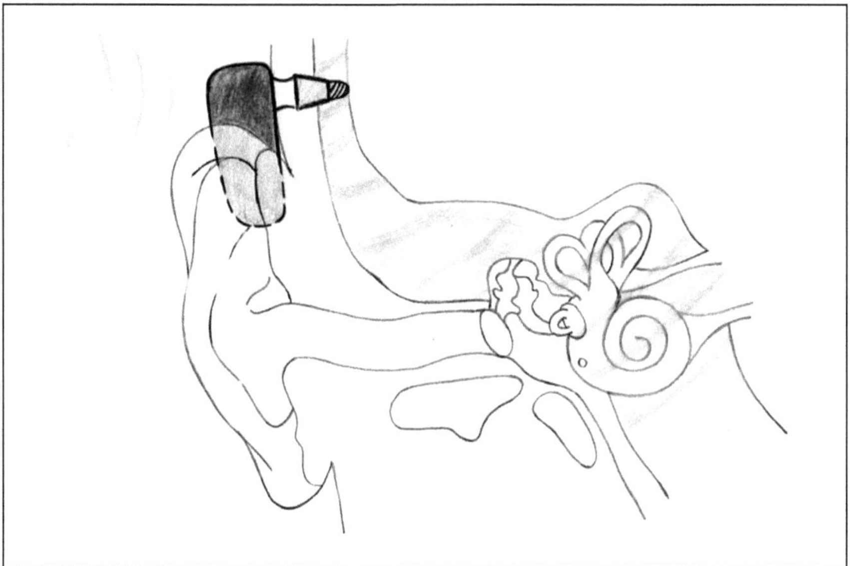

Figure 23: Bone anchored hearing aid.

The most powerful bone anchored hearing aids can be applied either to conductive or mixed hearing loss of up to 60 dB.[51] In case of one-sided deafness, they can be used as an alternative to CROS. In this instance, a BAHA system shall be positioned on the deaf side so that the sound transmitted via bone vibrations would reach and stimulate the cochlear located on the opposite side.[52]

A middle ear implant (Figure 24) is another solution for conductive hearing loss, specifically with otitis media and middle ear malformations.

It directly drives or replaces the middle ear bones in order to ensure that the sound is conducted to the cochlear. The external part of the middle ear implant system consists of a microphone, an amplifier, a signal processor, a coil and a battery. It is worn externally behind the ear. From this part, the processed sound is transferred to the implant located in the skull. It is done via the wireless connection established between the coils outside and inside the skull. The signal is then passed on to the transducers that transform the sound into vibrations and pass it to the cochlear.

51 Snik et al., 2005; Bosman et al., 2006.

52 Wazen et al., 2003; Snik et al., 2004; Stenfelt 2005.

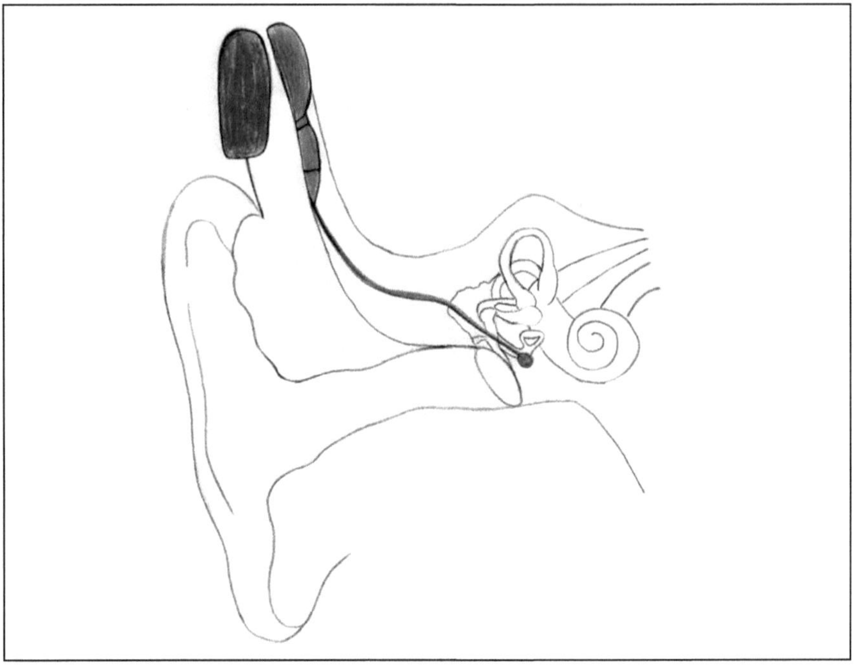

Figure 24: Middle ear implant.

Cochlear implants (Figure 25) were historically used only for two-sided inner ear deafness. Lately their application area has been increased to severe sensorineural hearing loss. Specifically, with the miniaturization of cochlear implants, increasingly more babies with hearing loss receive two-sided cochlear implants.

A cochlear implant system consists of an external part and an implant. The external part is located behind the ear and contains a microphone, an amplifier, a signal processor, a wireless coil, and a battery. The implant consists of a wireless coil, used to receive signals from the external part, and an electrode inserted into the cochlear. Depending on frequency of sound, the electrode stimulates different parts of cochlear basilar membrane.

If a patient still has the ability to understand low frequency sounds, a hybrid solution is possible. In such a solution, low frequency sounds are amplified and passed into the outer ear by a hearing instrument integrated into the external part of the cochlear implant. The high frequency sounds are transmitted via the electrode.[53]

53 Luetje et al, 2007.

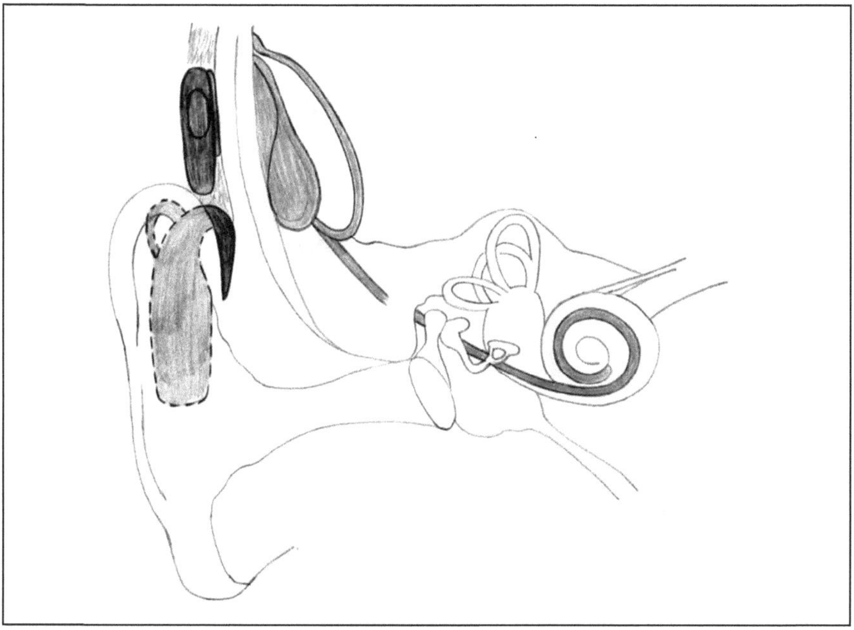

Figure 25: Cochlear implant.

In certain rare situations, even cochlear implants cannot help patients. This condition is called neural deafness. It occurs due to disruption of information transfer on the way between the cochlear and the brain. One of the causes of this condition is neurofibromatosis type II. This disease manifests itself with the development of symmetric, non-malignant brain tumors in the region of the auditory-vestibular nerve. The latter is responsible for transmitting sensory information from the inner ear to the brain. This disease is caused by mutations of the moesin-, ezrin-, radixin-like gene. Although tumors can be surgically removed, there is no therapy for underlying disorder of cell function caused by genetic mutation. In this case, an implant has to stimulate the central auditory system directly in the brain. Such an implant is called Auditory Brain Stimulation implant (Figure 26). Its external part is the same as that of a cochlear implant, but the implant part generates electrical stimulation of the auditory nerve, or replaces the auditory nerve with the electrode that goes straight into the brain.[54]

[54] Rosahl et al., 2004 ; Lenarz et al., 2006.

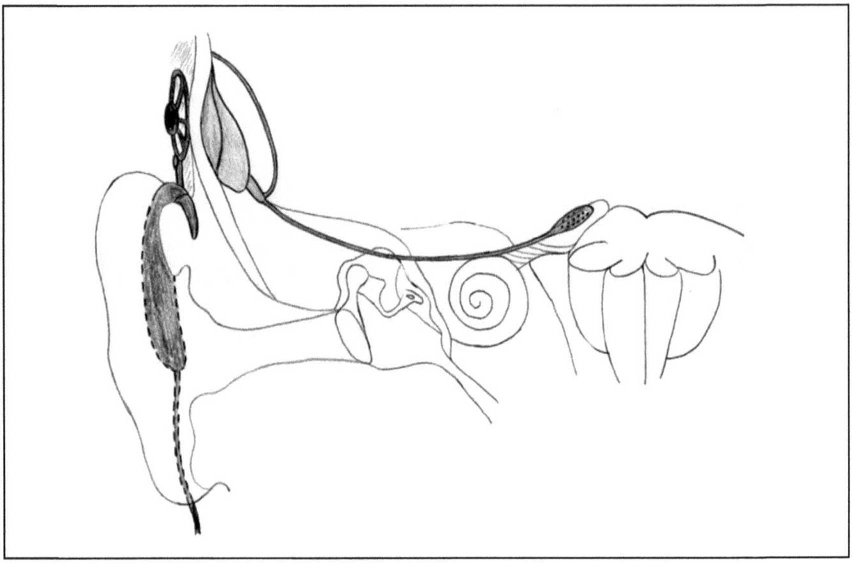

Figure 26: Auditory Brain Stimulation implant.

3 Literature Review on Financing Hearing Instruments and Implants Purchase

3.1 Lending from a Theoretical Perspective

The contemporary microfinance theory on lending to individuals is based on the works of Stiglitz (1990), and Ghatak and Guinnane (1999). Conning (2000) further expanded the theory. All these works describe lending in terms of the principal-agent model. Here, the lender is a principal, and the borrower is an agent. A principal delegates the authority to an agent to act on his behalf. In this case, it is to use the funds obtained via the loan on a project with the positive return on investment. The key risks for the principal associated with such interaction are the following:

- Adverse selection of borrowers at the time of loan disbursement. What kind of borrowers would like to borrow from a lender? How can a lender, using signaling mechanisms, influence decisions of potential borrowers to apply for a loan? If we have two types of borrowers – a safe type, and a risky one - a bank should be able to differentiate representatives of both types and vary interest rates for them in order to ensure profit. If the bank is not able to do that, adverse selection will occur. If an interest rate on a loan is comfortable for a safe borrower, both safe and risky borrowers will apply for a loan. Above that certain value of the interest rate, the safe borrower will leave the market, and only the risky borrower will stay. It is possible to make money even on the risky borrower, but then the interest rate has to be increased. This should be treated carefully as even the risky borrower would not be willing to take the loan above a certain interest rate.
- Moral hazard once a loan is granted, also known as ex-ante moral hazard. This is the borrower's moral hazard connected with the effort invested in a project. What will be the behavior of the borrower between the time when the loan is given and the repayment date? If a loan is made without collateral, or with collateral that is more valuable to the borrower than to the lender, the borrower, knowing that the real value of collateral is much lower than the loan, might decide to take on a riskier project than she/he has communicated to the lender. Additionally, in developing countries, where property rights and court systems are underdeveloped, the borrower might see a low practical risk of losing collateral in case of a default on the loan.

- Moral hazard once investment return has been realized, also known as ex-post moral hazard, e.g. will the borrower tell the truth to the lender about the outcome of the project? A bank might not know whether investment return is positive. In case of negative investment returns, meaning that the borrower has made less money at the end of the project than she/he has borrowed, and if the value of the available collateral does not cover the difference between investment proceeds and borrowed funds, the borrower might default. On the other hand, provided that the investment returns are positive, the borrower might still be interested in defaulting if the value of the collateral is much smaller than the value of the loan. If the borrower is liable only up to the value of collateral posted for a loan, an "information problem" emerges.

In case of borrowing to purchase a hearing instrument or an implant all the risks mentioned in the theoretical literature also apply:

- Adverse selection. Which hearing impaired should receive the loan and which should not? What are the criteria for differentiating between types of the hearing impaired? How can a lender ensure that a loan is given only to a person with hearing loss, who really wants to improve her/his quality of life?
- Ex-ante moral hazard. Will the borrower really spend the money on purchasing hearing instruments or implants, or will the borrower use the funds for other purposes? Will the hearing impaired be diligently wearing hearing instruments or will they just put them in the drawer? How can a lender make certain that the borrowed money is spent on hearing instruments or implants? How can a lender ensure that those hearing aids are put to use instead of just lying in the drawer?
- Ex-post moral hazard. Have the hearing instruments or the implants really helped the hearing impaired to hear better? Were the hearing impaired able to increase their income or integrate themselves better into the hearing society? How can a lender enforce the loan repayment at the end?

First, we explore the adverse selection risk. Potential borrowers of funds to purchase hearing instruments or implants differ in their ability to integrate into the hearing society, their preferences in terms of financing their hearing instruments or implants, and other characteristics that can affect their social integration. In modern literature, potential borrowers are described as individuals of various types. For example: "borrowers are risk-neutral and of two types, safe (a) and risky (b)."[1] The information about the borrower's type allows the lender to estimate risks associated with lending money to the borrower.

1 Ghatak & Guinnane, 1999, p. 201.

In a simple model, there are two types of potential borrowers: safe borrowers, and risky borrowers. The former are much more likely to have successful social integration with the help of aided hearing than the latter. An example of a risky borrower would be someone, who would value her/his hearing instrument or implant significantly lower than a safe borrower several months after fitting. Or it could be someone who uses the borrowed funds for other purposes (risky projects) than aided hearing. Such a borrower would be less willing to pay back the loan. Therefore, a lender would prefer to be able to differentiate between the two types of borrowers and tailor loan terms accordingly. In a perfect information world, this could be easily done. In a world of imperfect information, a lender has no other option but to offer a single set of contracts to both types.

Stiglitz and Weiss (1981) find that the interest rate a bank charges affects the riskiness of the pool of loans either by:

- Sorting potential borrowers (the adverse selection effect), or by
- Affecting the actions of borrowers (the incentive or ex-ante moral hazard effect).

In their study Stiglitz and Weiss (1981) show that there are no competitive forces leading supply to equal demand over the interest rate charged by lenders. With the growth of an interest rate charged on the loan above the level comfortable to safe borrowers but below a level necessary to compensate for risks incurred by risky borrowers, a lender will lose money. Safe borrowers will not be able to finance their projects on such a high interest rate. At the same time, the interest rate will not compensate for the risk caused by lending to risky borrowers. Consequently, in order to solve the under-investment problem, which exhibits itself in the need for safe borrowers to have interest rates below a certain level, Stiglitz and Weiss (1981) argue for the need for credit rationing in markets with imperfect information to allow safe borrowers to be financed.

For the hearing impaired, a lender needs to determine who will be satisfied with the aided hearing and, therefore, will benefit most from the loan. If it is not done properly, the adverse selection risk described above might occur. It could lead to the lender's losses on such loans, and, consequently, to the termination of the borrowing program for all hearing impaired.

One of the most widely used methods by Microfinance lenders to extract information about borrowers' types is Group Lending with Joint Liability. In a group lending, the loan is given to a group, rather than to an individual. Under the joint liability payment is understood a payment that needs to be done to cover the costs of a defaulting group member. Ghatak (1999) describes

> "... a theory based on two contractual features of group lending programs to explain why they can potentially achieve high repayment rates despite the fact that borrowers are not required to put in any collateral: the existence of joint liability and the selection

of group members by borrowers themselves. As mentioned above, screening potential loan applicants is a costly activity for the lender. At the same time, borrowers from the same locality are expected to have some information about each other's projects. Therefore, one way of looking at contracts based on self-formed groups is that they are a means of deliberately inducing borrowers to select their group members in a way that exploits this local information."[2]

To resolve the adverse selection problem Ghatak (2000) offers a method of screening potential borrowers for self-selection into different borrowing groups by differentiating interest rate and joint liability payments among group members.

"Under joint liability lending, the type of the partner matters only when the partner's project fails. Therefore, every borrower will prefer to have a safe partner because of lower expected joint liability payments. However, the benefit of having a safe rather than a risky partner is realized only when a borrower herself has succeeded. Hence a safe borrower is much more concerned about the type of her partner than a risky borrower, although both would prefer a safe partner."[3]

Therefore, safe borrowers would prefer to group with other safe borrowers for taking group loans with joint liability. Risky borrowers would be stuck with other risky borrowers. Because of the different value each type of borrowers assigns to having a safe partner, "lenders can exploit the degree of joint liability to screen borrowers with different (unobservable) probabilities of repayment."[4] Lenders can offer two types of contracts: one with low interest rate and high joint liability payment, and another with high interest rate and low joint liability payment.

"Risky borrowers, who fail and hence lose their collateral relatively more often, would self-select the latter while safe borrowers would select the former."[5]

Ghatak and Guinnane (1999) indicate the following reasons why joint-liability lenders outperform traditional banks regarding performance of loans to the poor:

- "members of a community may know more about one another … than an outside institution such as a bank."[6]
- "poor people's neighbors, on the other hand, may be able to impose powerful non-financial sanctions at low cost."[7]

---

2 Ghatak, 1999, p. 28.

3 Ghatak, 2000, pp. 609-610.

4 Ghatak, 2000, p. 602.

5 Ghatak, 2000, p. 625.

6 Ghatak & Guinnane, 1999, p. 197.

7 Ghatak & Guinnane, 1999, p. 197.

> "More generally, group lending derives its effectiveness from the social ties among potential group members. If those ties are weak, or if they imply an unwillingness to sanction one another ... the mechanism will not work."[8]

However, forming groups of the hearing impaired for lending with joint liability is unrealistic, as people with hearing loss are quite heterogeneous. Typically, they do not have strong enough social ties with each other to be able to sanction against each other effectively. Therefore, group lending with joint liability will not work for hearing impaired as a mechanism to reduce adverse selection. There is a need in another mechanism to protect lenders to the hearing impaired from adverse selection.

Next, we explore ex-ante moral hazard. There are two main ways of resolving moral hazard problems:

- Providing incentives to borrowers to align their interests with the interests of lenders;
- Monitoring actions taken by borrowers.

Ghatak and Guinnane (1999) recommend group lending with a joint liability as a way to ensure that the incentives of borrowers and lenders are aligned. Apart from the group lending, the main ways to influence borrower's incentives are either ensuring that the borrower does not want to use the borrowed funds for other purposes, or ensuring the borrower cannot use the borrowed funds for other purposes. The latter, in our case, can be achieved through channeling the borrowed funds directly to third parties who provide products and/or services to the hearing impaired. The former can be achieved by ensuring that the hearing impaired are confident that they can benefit from aided hearing.

Second, let us take a look at monitoring actions taken by the borrower. Practically, it is quite difficult for a lender to do the monitoring herself/himself due to the high cost of monitoring. On the other hand, group lending with joint liability offers the monitoring possibility by peers of a borrower at a low cost. If group lending is not possible, some other mechanisms shall be used.

A hearing impaired person has a choice between wearing diligently the hearing aids, or using them only occasionally and enjoying some private benefit. This private benefit can come in a form of rest from wearing hearing instruments. Therefore, if a hearing impaired person is confident that using hearing aids on a regular basis is in her/his own interests, the private benefit will diminish, and there will be less need in monitoring borrower's actions.

Next, we explore ex-post moral hazard. As we all know, borrowers can voluntary or involuntary default. Involuntary default means that the outcome of the project undertaken by the borrower is not sufficient to cover the loan repayment.

---

8 Ghatak & Guinnane, 1999, p. 221.

For the hearing impaired person this signifies that she/he is not any better integrated into the hearing society now than before the loan. Therefore, she/he may not be able to pay back the loan. Thus, it is very important to differentiate between borrowers and give loans only to those hearing impaired, who can significantly benefit from aided hearing to be able to pay back loans.

A hearing impaired person can also default voluntarily. Voluntary default means that the outcome of the project undertaken by the borrower is sufficient to cover the loan repayment; nevertheless, the borrower decides to default on the loan. In our case, this means that the hearing impaired person is significantly better integrated into the hearing society due to aided hearing, has sufficient money to pay back the loan, but is not willing to do so. In this instance, it is important to give the borrower strong enough incentives to pay back the loan. An example of such an incentive can be the risk of losing collateral posted on the loan.

Although both defaults should be avoided, it is inefficient to punish a borrower, who defaults involuntarily. Therefore, the ability to differentiate between the voluntary and involuntary default is crucial for the lender.

3.2 Group Lending versus Individual Lending

Group lending has been one of the main success factors behind Microfinance in developing countries, because it allows introducing economies of scale, and saving on screening, monitoring and enforcing. Nevertheless, the recent evidence shows that group lending *per se* is not always the optimal solution.

> "Unless group members can impose costly social sanctions on one another, or unless the bank uses cross-reporting mechanisms group lending may do worse than individual lending" [9]

Besides, "cross-reporting increases the bargaining power of unsuccessful borrowers, and is robust to collusion against the bank". [10]

Armendariz de Aghion and Morduch (2000) speak about the "new programmes"[11] for individual-based lending. These new programmes

> "... have demonstrated the advantages of employing individual-based contracts instead of only using group lending contracts. Unlike the group lending programmes, these new programmes require borrowers to put up collateral or find a third-party guarantor, and they serve a better-off group of clients. But unlike with standard borrower-lender

9 Bhole & Ogden, 2010, p. 348.

10 Rai & Sjöström, 2004, p. 217.

11 Armendariz de Aghion & Morduch, 2000, p. 418.

relashionships, the new banks use novel means to collect information and to create incentives for timely loan repayment."[12]

Gené and Karlan (2011) confirm this in their practical experiment. The experiment took place in multiple lending centers. "Typically a lending center starts with 15-30 individuals residing in the same barangay (community)."[13] The experiment "was conducted on the island of Leyte, and all 169 centers on the island were included".[14] In this experiment Gené and Karlan (2011)

> "... randomly converted existing centers with group liability loans to individual liability loans. All other aspects of the program remained the same (including attendance at center meetings and weekly payment made in groups). Clients were not told this was an experiment, and thus had no information from the bank to suggest that a failure to repay could lead to a reversal of the change. The only two features that changed are the group liability and the savings rules. By removing the group liability, no member is held liable for another member's default. Thus, members are no longer forced to contribute towards the repayment of other members in default and no longer required to sign as co-maker of others' loans."[15]

The result of the experiment was that "individual liability compared to group liability leads to no change in repayment".[16]

We see from the experiment described in Gené and Karlan (2011) that individual lending, when exercised with caution to ensure proper checks and balances against adverse selection and moral hazard, is at least not a worse option than group lending. Group lending is typically used when there is a tightly knit group of people, like neighbors in a village, where each individual needs a loan for a similar purpose – typically income generating self-employment activities. While, as mentioned above, self-employment is also an attractive proposition for the hearing impaired, their first immediate need is the inclusion in the hearing society and economy through aiding their hearing impairment. Therefore, due to this additional significant requirement for funding, the hearing impaired cannot be easily included into the typically homogeneous neighborhood lending group involved in microfinancing.

In addition, the hearing impaired typically are not concentrated in the same geographical area like a small village, but rather are dispersed, and are a quite heterogeneous group of people, differentiated from each other by gender, age, income level, physical and intellectual abilities etc. Thus, forming a sustainable group of the hearing impaired for group loans is often impossible.

---

12 Armendariz de Aghion & Morduch, 2000, p. 418.

13 Gené & Karlan, 2011, p. 9.

14 Gené & Karlan, 2011, p. 9.

15 Gené & Karlan, 2011, pp. 10-11.

16 Gené & Karlan, 2011, p. 29.

3.3 Funding Medical Devices Purchases

Daher and Fessa (2010) investigate the need for Microfinance as a tool for financing wheelchairs and oxygen concentrators for patients with chronic lung diseases.

> "The majority, i.e., 89% of the patients with a walking disability and 95% of the patients with a chronic lung disease, believed that microfinance would be an ideal tool for them to finance these devices and that they or their family could pay back the installments."[17]

Nevertheless, the study shows that Microfinance, so far, did not play any significant role in helping people with disabilities in Syria to buy medical devices they need:

> "Of the patients, 24.4% suffering from a walking disability and 22% with chronic lung diseases had ever been in contact with a microfinance institution. However, they had not received credit for medical devices, but for "normal" activities in the traditional field of business in microfinance institutions, such as financing the start-up of a grocery store."[18]

The study concludes that unfortunately

> "... people who are prevented from working because they cannot afford a medical device have no access to the financial services offered on the market. Traditional banking services are not accessible to the poor, and microfinance organizations fear that these people cannot pay back their credits."[19]

This finding is consistent with the earlier similar experience from microfinance for women with disabilities in Zambia and Zimbabwe (Lewis, 2004). Lewis (2004) outlines the barriers women with disabilities in Zambia and Zimbabwe face to obtain microfinancing.

> "Indeed, each of the few women, who had at some point applied for small business loans outside of disability organizations had been turned down, either explicitly on the basis of disability, or because she had been unable to produce the collateral required of disabled, but not of non-disabled credit applicants."[20]

> "Disabled women may have children and other dependents, whom they need to feed, clothe, and educate, just as do their nondisabled sisters. But, because of their comparatively low market value as wives, women with disabilities are more likely than their non-disabled counterparts to be unmarried mothers, or to have been abandoned. Girls

---

17 Daher & Fessa, 2010, p. 189.

18 Daher & Fessa, 2010, p. 193.

19 Daher & Fessa, 2010, p. 195.

20 Lewis, 2004, p. 34.

with disabilities are frequently a family's last priority for scarce educational resources, and have less access to educational or vocational training programmes which would prepare them for the job market"[21]

Women with disabilities in Zimbabwe face such barriers to obtain microfinance as "stigma related to disability, and the resulting discrimination in training, loan opportunities, and the marketplace."[22] Lewis (2004) shows that women with disabilities are often perceived as high risk, and thus refused the loans.

> "Microfinance lenders commonly share the prejudices against women with disabilities that lead to this exclusion. They assume that, by virtue of their disability, women with disabilities are not appropriate for microcredit or business services, or that they are adequately and better served by rehabilitation programmes and charities." [23]

Nevertheless, depending on the degree of solidarity feeling in a given culture, disabled entrepreneurs might "benefit" from solidarity feeling of other people and compassion towards the disability. Depending on the culture, some customers might choose to buy from or do business with a disabled person. Depending on the culture and family, relatives and family members of a disabled person might actually be providing significant help to the disabled family member, trying to boost his/her self-esteem. In such cases, running one's own business might be even easier for a disabled person than for a non-disabled person without the network of helping relatives.

Health insurance plays only a minor role in coverage of medical devices costs for poor people, since many of them do not have the necessary health insurance, or the insurance policy provides only rudimentary support for medical devices purchase. Boutayeb (2006) carried out a study in Morocco and showed that health insurance plays a minor role, and it covers only 16% of the entire population. Even in the United Stated, the majority of hearing instruments are purchased without any government or insurance reimbursement.[24] Thus, it is difficult for the hearing impaired poor people in the developing countries to rely on health insurance in terms of financing their hearing aids.

The Starkey Hearing Foundation, by far the largest non-profit organization active in charity for the hearing impaired, is committed to provide 100,000 hearing aids worldwide every year. Compared to around 360 million people worldwide with moderate to profound hearing impairment[25], we can see that charity organizations help an extremely small portion of the hearing impaired.

---

[21] Lewis, 2004, p. 31.

[22] Lewis, 2004, p. 31.

[23] Lewis, 2004, p. 31.

[24] Kochkin, 2007.

[25] World Health Organization, 2013.

Daher and Fessa (2010) point out that in addition to the cost of a medical device itself, there are maintenance costs that a disabled person has to cover in order to ensure functioning of the device. In case of hearing instruments this would be the price for batteries, ear domes, wind screens, head phones, out-of-warranty repairs etc. - depending on the type and model of a hearing instrument. Thus, the hearing impaired people also need money for maintenance of their hearing aids.

> “Asymmetric information between microfinance institutions and the disabled population is probably the main hindrance for increased penetration of microcredit services to disabled persons.”[26]

In particular, Mersland (2005) points to the importance of the correct structure of the loan repayment for disabled people. “Loans are in general best suited for ongoing businesses.”[27]

> “Microcredit for disabled persons should normally target persons with existing businesses with positive cash flows. Such businesses may be ongoing business as shops, small farms etc. held by disabled persons.”[28]

Mersland (2005) argues that if a loan for the purchase of a medical device is structured like a standard consumer loan and not properly aligned with cash inflows of a self-employed disabled person, it can lead to default on the loan.

He gives an example of a disabled person, who wants to start a business of producing and selling milk from a cow, and takes a loan for purchasing a calf. It is important to realize that it might take more than a year for a calf to grow up and be able to give milk. Therefore, financing such a venture with a four months loan with fixed monthly installments would not be a good idea.

> “This means that if persons with disabilities are to get loans from most MFIs they should be involved in businesses that produce an immediate income stream allowing for starting to pay installments within 1-4 weeks.”[29]

In addition, Mersland (2005) points to the fact that

> “For more risky investments (where repayment rates are lower due to higher probability of bankruptcy), equity is more common. Thus, equity finance is normally needed for new ventures, new product developments, research etc.”[30]

---

26 Mersland, 2005, p. 2.

27 Mersland, 2005, p. 22.

28 Mersland, 2005, p. 23.

29 Mersland, 2005, p. 23.

30 Mersland, 2005, p. 23.

A project of financing hearing aids for a hearing impaired person without any current income with the goal of repayment of the initial investment after a hearing impaired person starts making income with aided hearing is an example of such a risky investment. Although, it is difficult to imagine how equity financing could work practically for financing a hearing aid purchase, but the findings of Mersland (2005) and Daher and Fessa (2010) point to the limitations of the traditional microfinance loans or consumer loans in the case of serving people with disabilities and no income.

A financial institution that participates in financing medical devices purchases for disabled faces the risk of payment enforcement. Although payment enforcement and collateral collection are standard practices in banking and finance, the traditional payment enforcement applied to disabled individuals might damage the reputation of the lender. Despite the fact that it is possible to design a solution to cover this risk, the financial institution has to remember that, besides loans, there are also savings, insurance, cash transfers and other services it can use. These services might not only directly benefit disabled individuals, but also help them to purchase a needed medical device without taking on a debt burden.

Depending on the type and degree of hearing loss, the hearing impaired require different hearing instruments. In the developing countries, the cost of the simplest digital trimmer device is around 160 USD. Such devices are acceptable in many hearing loss cases for one-on-one conversations in a quiet environment. In discussions with background noise or for group conversations, computer programmed devices with directional speech focus starting at 400 USD per piece are required. Besides, binaural fitting is necessary for around 80% of all hearing impaired. This makes the total cost of aided hearing to be around 320-800 USD. In addition, hearing instrument batteries normally last only a week when the hearing aid is used 16 hours per day. The performance will vary slightly depending on the style and type of hearing aid technology. Batteries cost approximately 4 USD per month. For many households in the developing countries finding 320-800 USD needed for the purchase of hearing aids can be a real challenge.

The known sources of funding the purchase of hearing instruments are savings by a hearing impaired person or her/his family, government or medical insurance reimbursements, charity grants, insurance, and loans. As hearing loss disability, presence of comorbidities, a family situation, educational level, and an individual income differ among the hearing impaired, there are no one-fits-all rules for funding hearing aid purchases, like there is no one-fits-all hearing aid.

Loans given to the hearing impaired have the same fundamental risks as consumer loans to people without disabilities. As mentioned above, these risks are adverse selection, ex-ante moral hazard and ex-post moral hazard.

Traditional microfinance suggests group lending or its modifications such as cross-reporting and peer monitoring to minimize these risks. The group lending approach helps to solve adverse selection, ex-ante moral hazard, and ex-post moral hazard. However, as noticed above, it is hard to form a sustainable group of the hearing impaired for successful group loans. Even if such a group were created, it would have to include only neighbors or close relatives in order for ex-ante and ex-most moral hazard prevention mechanisms to work. As such, this is not a workable solution.

Daher and Fessa (2010) came to the conclusion that in order for the micro-finance loans to people with disabilities to be approved and able to function properly, the borrowers have to be willing to become self-employed after the purchase of the necessary medical devices.

> "One possibility of credit repayment is for the recipient to become self-employed. It is assumed that after the acquisition of the necessary medical devices, the credit user will be able to start up his or her own business. With the realized profit, the credits can be repaid. The results of the investigation show that a large number of the patients suffering from a walking disability (68.7%) completely agreed that they could conduct small independent projects with a small loan despite their physical disability if they possessed a wheelchair."[31]

This indicates that individual lending for people with disabilities is not a bad solution under certain circumstances. It offers maximum flexibility in designing the loan terms to meet the needs of people with hearing loss, but still needs to mitigate the three main risks associated with the loans – adverse selection, ex-ante and ex-post moral hazard.

3.4 Individual Lending

Many individual lending programs offered by banks and other credit institutions require periodic loan repayments starting almost immediately after the loan disbursement. If a hearing impaired person has a stable cash flow either from gainful employment, or from entrepreneurship, such programs can be considered. These loans are similar to standard consumer loans for consumer electronics purchase. They look attractive to some people because of their strong bias towards the present compared to the future. It is natural to have some sort of present-bias due to the time value of money– a dollar today is worth more than a dollar tomorrow. To calculate how much more the money is worth today than in the future, interest rates are used. If a hearing impaired person discounts in her/his mind future cash flow stronger than a lender, she/he will be more interested in taking a loan to buy hearing aids now than saving for the needed purchase.

---

[31] Daher & Fessa, 2010, pp. 193-194.

When giving a loan to a person with hearing loss, it would be wise to allow her/him start paying back the loan after aural rehabilitation is completed, not immediately after the loan disbursement. This allows the borrower time to better integrate in the hearing society, and perhaps increase her/his income. However, it is difficult to predict time the hearing impaired individual needs to get used to hearing aids. It depends on personal characteristics and age of a user, the type and technological level of purchased hearing aids, skills of hearing aids dispenser, etc. Therefore, this approach to loans is not acceptable for lending organizations as delay in loan repayments leads to high level of ex-post moral hazard. On the other hand, standard consumer loans with a fixed repayment schedule help to minimize the ex-ante and ex-post moral hazard, and as a result are popular among lenders.

A standard consumer loan will work when a person has sudden adult onset hearing loss caused by trauma or side-effects of medications, but does not have money for hearing aid purchase. It is an especially good option when the same adult had a gainful employment before the hearing loss and has strong reasons to believe that given the restored hearing ability she/he can regain her/his level of income. A standard consumer loan is also a good solution when an active hearing instrument user wants to purchase a new hearing instrument instead of the one he/she is using now. In these cases, the brain cells responsible for processing hearing information are still in place and aural rehabilitation will be quick. This often implies that the adult will be able to return to work and pay back the loan. Another reason for success of standard consumer loans when dealing with sudden adult onset hearing loss is that psychological comorbidities associated with hearing loss did not have time to develop. Therefore, the self-confidence of the hearing impaired is still approximately on the same level it used to be before hearing loss occurred.

On the other hand, if hearing loss is not sudden and has developed slowly through a long period of time, several years perhaps, and during all this time it was unaided, aural rehabilitation will be an important part of the process of the hearing impaireds' inclusion in the society. In such a situation, a person with hearing loss might have gradually lost many of her/his friends and connections, and developed comorbidities of psychological nature like, for example, identity crisis, depression etc. A quick improvement in the quality of person's life is not expected. Thus, if a hearing impaired person does not have money immediately available for the hearing aid purchase, a consumer loan is not recommended. The only workable solution in these instances for a person with hearing loss is to save the necessary sum and/or consider other low-risk sources of funding the purchase such as government or charity funding, or help from family members.

3.5 Rent and Hire Purchase

Many hearing impaired have low self-esteem, feel incompetent and inadequate due to the stigma associated with hearing loss and rejections they suffer in everyday life. They often experience depression, sadness, nervousness, anxiety, isolation and frequently a sense of guilt for unsuccessful communication and misunderstandings. The interviews I conducted with the hearing impaired showed that they are often afraid of making a financial commitment that they might not be able to meet. Therefore, they are frequently wary of taking a loan for hearing aids purchase. In such instances, hearing aids rent can be a possible solution. Rental programs are designed to make hearing instruments affordable to a number of people. This way a person with hearing loss can test various hearing aids and find the one that suits her/him best without giving away a fortune. Unfortunately, renting without collateral works only in well-developed countries where a hearing instrument owner can exercise some control over the renter's actions in case of neglecting or loosing the hearing instrument, not returning it on time, or failing to make rental payments. In developing countries, the owner should probably take collateral. The problem is that hearing instrument dispensers are not pawnbrokers, and as a result are not in the position to assess the value of the physical goods offered as collateral. They cannot become pawnbrokers, because being a pawnbroker is a completely different business model from being a hearing instrument dispenser. Pawnbrokers need to be able to assess the value of collateral, sell it efficiently, store the items, and enforce payments. Besides, in Russia and Ukraine pawnbrokers are widely available. A hearing instrument dispenser can always refer the hearing impaired to the nearest one if needed. Thus, for hearing aid dispensers taking physical items like livestock, gold rings, cell phones or home appliances as collateral on hearing aid rent would be inefficient.

There are only a couple of reasons why a person with hearing loss would prefer renting to owning:

- She/he has mild hearing loss and needs hearing aids only temporarily - for example to go to a job interview
- She/he wants to test different types of hearing instruments to make sure she/he buys the right one later

There is every reason to believe that when the hearing impaired do have money for hearing aids purchase, they will use it to obtain the needed devices, and will not spend it on other discretional consumption. Besides, they will prefer buying, not renting, as the former will give them a sense of permanency. On top of that, it is now possible to buy a digital trimmer hearing instrument only for 160 USD.

On the other hand, for a large number of years rent will always be more expensive than just a standard loan for purchase of hearing instruments due to the need to compensate the rental risk.

Nevertheless, for the sake of discussion, let us take a look at rent where a third party (relative, friend, family member) pledges for a hearing impaired person. If a renter defaults, a pledger would have to pay back the value of missed rental payments to a dispenser. The rented devices have to be returned. If they are not returned, their full price has to be paid. In case of loan default, a pledger has to pay only the outstanding debt and interest. The needed hearing aids remain with the hearing impaired. Thus, it will make more sense to a pledger to pledge for a loan.

In addition, hearing aid rent is limited to certain types of hearing instruments. Because of high upfront cost and almost zero resale value, it will not work for implants or any kind of custom-made aids. BTE, OTE, RIC and pocket aid devices might have to be refurbished first in order to be offered in a next renting transaction.

Besides, many hearing aid dispensers are not interested to offer hearing aid rent service due to high transaction costs, need to refurbish and high income only in the long run.

The only alternative to a standard consumer loan that one can see in practice so far is the hire purchase. In Ukraine and Lithuania, hearing aid dispensers offer a hire purchase of hearing instruments. This means that 70% of the hearing aid cost is paid during the first fitting session, and the remaining 30% is paid in 3 installments within a 3 months period. This is in effect a form of a consumer loan with a hearing aid dispenser playing a role of a bank. Not all dispensers are willing to do this. Besides, for the hearing impaired who have funds available that cover less than 70% of the hearing aids cost and/or have no stable income to ensure the payment of the remaining 30%, this also is not an acceptable option.

3.6 Savings

Saving is an increase in assets over a period of time. An asset is an economic resource that an individual, a company or a country owns or controls in hope for future benefits. It can be converted into cash. Money is also considered to be an asset. Correspondingly, income is an inflow of resources. When people receive their income, they can either spend it on consumption, or save for the future. Once a person consumes the saved resources, the dissaving occurs.

Assets can take various forms. They can be liquid monetary savings, such as cash and checking accounts, or less liquid, like cars, homes, clothes, furniture, home appliances etc. In developing countries, savings can also be in form of livestock or food. The least liquid assets include human capital (education, training, skills), and social capital (trust, network). Regardless of their form, assets help to smooth consumption, make large purchases and buffer risk.

Accumulating assets can help the hearing impaired to purchase a hearing aid and pay rehabilitation period expenses. For them it is the lowest risk finance tool. It is especially true for the hearing impaired who need a long rehabilitation period in order to get used to understanding speech via hearing aids. They will not have to face penalties for not meeting their financial obligations as in case of loans.

Multiple theories describe people's saving behavior:

- Economic theory suggests that people are rational human beings seeking to maximize their long-term benefit.[32] "The individual at a point of time is assumed to be both a farsighted planner and a myopic doer."[33] In economic theory, individuals are constantly deciding between saving and consumption. Modigliani (1966) and Friedman (1957) assume that people discount their consumption and future income. This helps them to decide what part of their lifetime recourses is to spend now and what part is to save for later.
- Social/psychological theory relaxes the assumptions of economic theory by admitting that preferences are not always rational. Not only society, but also "information, access, incentives, and facilitation"[34] influence an individual's saving ability. For example, Lusardi (2001) discovered that people who see their family and friends save are more likely to save themselves.
- Behavorial theory recognizes that people have mental accounts of their assets. Besides, they are more willing to consume current income rather than the future one.[35] People might be comfortable to take a loan to buy a home or pursue a college education, but not comfortable with debt to finance their daily expenses, such as food and clothing. The most important insight of the behavorial theory is that people can be both long-term oriented and myopic at the same time. Therefore, many people prefer saving solutions, where they get rewards for savings.[36]

One of the limitations of the economic and social theories is that they assume time-consistency of the discount rate of individuals. O'Donahue and Rabin

---

32 Thaler & Shefrin, 1981.

33 Thaler & Shefrin, 1981, p. 392.

34 Beverly & Sherraden, 1999, p. 40.

35 Shefrin & Thaler, 1988.

36 Thaler, 1994; Maital, 1986.

(1999) give the following example to illustrate time-inconsistency of the discount rate of individuals:

> "For example, when presented a choice between doing seven hours of an unpleasant activity on April 1 versus eight hours on April 15, if asked on February 1 virtually everyone would prefer the seven hours on April 1. But come April 1, given the same choice, most of us are apt to put off the work until April 15."[37]

What we see here is that an individual discounts long-term pay-offs at a lower discount rate, than the short term pay-offs. This phenomenon is also called hyperbolic discounting, because the function representing such time-inconsistency has a hyperbolic shape.

Hyperbolic discounting is an important part of the behavioral theory.[38] Because of the present-bias caused by hyperbolic discounting, many individuals would benefit from financial vehicles that help them make commitments to the future. Applying behavioral theory deductively to the hearing impaired (as a subset of total population), we can conclude that many hearing impaired also discount their future cash flows hyperbolically. They put excessively high weight on consumption today comparing to consumption of the future periods. Consequently, saving for such hearing impaired is quite a challenge. According to the behavioral theory they have strong intrisic incentives to consume today rather than later. On the other hand, according to economic theory, saving for hearing aids purchase is rational choice as aided hearing increases long-term well-being of the hearing impaired. Behavior theory points to the fact that subjective discount rates might prevent the hearing impaired from saving.

Escaping poverty requires asset accumulation. It is important to do something to help the hearing impaired to save for aided hearing rather than consume all available income immediately. Both developing and developed countries have their set of solutions used to reward savings and punish dissavings as per behavioral theory. In developed countries, these are all kinds of payroll deductions, time deposits, and education savings accounts. For example, payroll deduction 401(k) in the US removes payday temptation to spend money that goes into the retirement account. On the other hand, time deposits help people stick to their saving plans by offering a penalty for early withdrawal.

Poor and unbanked households in the US use such commitment saving devices as postponing to cash paychecks, giving money to a trusted person for safekeeping, refusing to have an ATM card, opening a bank account in an inconveniently located branch, and choosing savings accounts that charge per withdrawal.[39]

---

[37] O'Donahue & Rabin, 1999, p. 103.

[38] O'Donahue & Rabin, 1999; Laibson, 1997; Thaler, 1990; Lowenstein & Thaler, 1989.

[39] Beverly et al., 2003.

In developing countries, one of the commitment saving devices is ROSCA (Rotating Saving and Credit Association). It is a group of people. They meet frequently and make regular contributions to a fund. Each member can take a lump sum when needed. Every time a different group member receives the money. Some ROSCAs have spending agreements, which limit the use of funds. Health spending agreements of ROSCAs result in a significant increase of investments in preventative health products.[40]

Another commitment saving device used in the developing countries is the personalized deposit collection. Here, a deposit collector comes to visit a depositor at home in a defined time interval. This service does not come cheap, but still a lot of people are willing to pay for it. The main reason is that such collection works as a reminder and moral pressure to save.

Collins et al. (2009) give one more example of a commitment saving device:

> "In a slum in Vijayawada, a town in southern India, Seema negotiated a loan of $20 from a moneylender, at 15 percent a month, just after leaving a meeting of her local savings cooperative where she had $55 in a liquid savings account. This struck us as an expensive, perhaps even an irrational choice. But asked why she had done it, Seema said, "Because at this interest rate I know I'll pay back the loan money very quickly. If I withdrew my savings it would take me a long time to rebuild the balance.""[41]

Saving for the hearing impaired to buy aided hearing is the financial tool with the lowest risk. Our quantitative research in Russia and Ukraine shows that many hearing impaired are either impatient or have hyperbolic time preferences. Therefore, it is important to provide incentives and infrastructure that encourage savings. On the other hand, the faster a hearing impaired person gets a hearing aid, the shorter is the needed rehabilitation period. As mentioned above, each case of hearing impairment is unique. In some cases, waiting until a sufficient sum to buy a hearing aid builds up is not the best option. Nevertheless, savings is an important component of sustainable financing for aided hearing. The fact is, hearing instruments or implants processors need to be renewed once in several years. Therefore, for the hearing impaired, it is essential to have access to the appropriate savings infrastructure.

[40] Dupas & Robinson, 2013.

[41] Collins et al., 2009, pp. 110-111.

4 Qualitative Research on the Healthcare Economic Policy for Hearing Impairment

4.1 Research Methodology

The first part of this research is based on the qualitative study of the hearing impaired in Russia and Ukraine. It involves in-depth understanding of their behavior, the reasons behind why and how they make their decisions. We research their psychology and educational level, hearing prosthesis technology, consumer finance, microfinance, government policy, capacity of charitable organizations etc.

The qualitative research approach enables us to collect relevant detailed information about the hearing impaired and their environment. It gives us deep understanding of the hearing impaired behavior, how they perceive their surroundings and what influences their decisions. It builds a strong empirical foundation for the quantitative research we use later to confirm the findings from the qualitative research.

Glaser and Strauss (1967) gave the description of grounded theory to be used in qualitative research. Later, Strauss and Corbin (1998) updated it indicating that many techniques like interviews, case study research, questionnaires and observations should be used.

The first part of my research follows the grounded theory building approach. The goal is to generate explicit theory on social inclusion of the hearing impaired through financing their hearing instruments or implants.

Qualitative research uses an interpretive, naturalistic approach and studies phenomena in environments where they occur naturally.[1] Besides, qualitative research looks at how the social experience is created and given meaning.[2] Van Maanen (1998) points out to the "flexibility and emergent character"[3] of qualitative research and the need for "highly contextualized individual judgment"[4] when conducting one. According to him, qualitative research is inductive and interpretive. Therefore, this research is executed inductively by interpreting observations and constructing theory from events observed, read or heard about, results of questionnaires and interviews.

---

1 Denzin & Lincoln, 1994.

2 Denzin & Lincoln, 2005.

3 Van Maanen, 1998, p. xi.

4 Van Maanen, 1998, p. xi.

4.2 Research Setting and Data Collection

Qualitative research was carried out in form of observations, discussions and interviews. The interviews with hearing impaired people took place in Russia and Ukraine. Since hearing aid industry is global, in addition interviews with audiologists, hearing instrument manufacturers, hearing instrument distributors, organizations of the hearing impaired, microfinance and consumer finance organizations, lawyers were conducted in different countries including Zambia, Bangladesh, India, Ukraine, Germany, USA, Brazil, Singapore, Indonesia and Russia. Moreover, a two week research trip to Ukraine was made. Although the information was received from different countries, the focus was on the hearing impaired in countries like Russia and Ukraine where healthcare reimbursement policies are not sufficient to ensure that the majority of the hearing impaired get hearing aids.

The empirical data was collected during the 18-month research between October 2010 and April 2012. The primary sources of data collection were participant's observations, surveys, literature on hearing impairment, consumer finance and microfinance, and interviews. 47 interviews were performed with 35 different persons. Each one lasted from half an hour to an hour.

After having collected the empirical data, it was categorized into several main categories. These categories form the skeleton on which qualitative theory was built with the help of the grounded theory approach.

4.3 Findings

As a result of qualitative research, key factors behind optimally financing social inclusion of the hearing impaired were identified:

- A hearing impaired person has to be willing to integrate into the normal-hearing society with the help of a hearing instrument or an implant;
- Depending on the personal situation, 2 main approaches or a combination of them should be considered to finance a hearing instrument or an implant:
  a) Borrow;
  b) Save.

The first factor can be absent for various reasons. Most common are the following:

- A hearing impaired person does not see how aided hearing can help her/him to be better off. She/he does not realize that aided hearing can help her/him to obtain skills or knowledge needed to earn a higher income or in any other way enjoy a higher quality of life;

- A hearing impaired person did not use her/his hearing sense to communicate for a long period of time, sometimes never. She/he feels excluded from the normal-hearing society and/or is already strongly integrated in the society of the unaided hearing impaired. There they use means other than speech, for example sign language, to communicate with each other;
- A hearing impaired person uses the hearing sense only occasionally in a quiet environment without any outside pressure. She/he has already distanced herself/himself from the rest of the society and leads a rather secluded life;
- A hearing impaired person has a strong prejudice against hearing implants.

To start with, we take a closer look at the first reason. Here, the driver behind the lack of interest in social inclusion with the help of aided hearing is the absence of skills or knowledge required to earn a higher income and enjoy a higher quality of life. In some cases, the hearing impaired do not even feel that they need the additional ability (hearing) as they can perform certain physical work and earn income despite their hearing loss. For example, some people with severe unaided hearing loss in Ukraine perform the market trading. Their neighbors from the market help them to speak with customers to complete sales. The hearing impaired, in exchange, look after the goods of these neighbors. Besides, such physical activities like carpentry, construction, repair work, house painting, cleaning and many factory jobs can also be done by people with unaided hearing loss. Therefore, hearing loss *per se* does not prohibit the hearing impaired to carry out simple physical labor. Still, there is a significant range of activities that involve verbal interaction with other people and are extremely challenging for a person with unaided hearing loss. In these instances, hearing instruments help to acquire the missing knowledge and lead a more fulfilling life.

The second reason behind the lack of interest in social inclusion is the absence of hearing sense for a long time. A hearing aid adjustment period is much more complex than an adjustment period for glasses. If a visually impaired person, even without prior experience, gets the glasses, she/he can immediately see much better. Her/his quality of life improves right away. In case of hearing aids, it is not that simple. With every passing day, sensory deprivation of the human brain increases. Under the term sensory deprivation we understand that brain cells responsible for processing information coming from hearing sense have not been used for a defenite time period. The length of sensory deprivation is the time a person had hearing loss but did not use hearing aids for amplification.

Ching et al. (1998) introduced the term effective audibility. It determines the level of amplification, at which no additional information gets extracted from the sound signal by a hearing impaired person. Due to sensory deprivation, no new information can be processed by the brain of a hearing impaired person above the level of effective audibility. This means that when a first time hearing aid user is fitted with a hearing aid, it does not make sense to give the incoming sound the level of amplification equal to hearing loss. Effective audibility for the first time users can be as low as 30-40% of the incoming speech. This implies that the hearing impaired fitted with a hearing instrument for the first time will not be able to understand up to 60-70% of the incoming speech.

As a hearing impaired person gets used to wearing a hearing instrument, her/his brain adapts to process incoming audial information. The need to adjust the amplification level of a hearing impaired to her/his new audibility level arises.[5] The process of fine-tuning a hearing aid, and training the brain to process higher effective audibility rate information is called aural rehabilitation.

Aural rehabilitation helps the hearing impaired to understand the limits of sound amplification and minimize the negative effects of hearing loss on communication with other people.[6] Despite the proven outcomes of aural rehabilitation, even in developed countries aural rehabilitation services are rarely used. Kochkin (1993) noted the scarcity of post-hearing instrument fitting rehabilitative services in the US and suggested that this may be the main reason behind poor understanding of the perceived benefit from amplification by individuals with hearing loss. In the developing countries, aural rehabilitation is even rarer. Given the scarcity of aural rehabilitation, time can serve as its substitute. Time is necessary for the hearing impaired to get used to amplification, wearing hearing devices and to learn to communicate effectively using hearing aids. The collected evidence suggests that for a person first fitted with a hearing aid, the amount of time needed for rehabilitation approximately equals the time it took hearing loss to develop from normal hearing to pre-fitting level. The rehabilitation period often lasts several years. In the US, the average time between the moment a patient first experienced hearing loss and a hearing aid purchase is 6 years.

If a hearing impaired person has a sudden adult-onset hearing loss caused, for example, by trauma, disease or medication side-effects, and is fitted with the hearing aid relatively quickly after the occurrence, she/he will have a short rehabilitation period. In this case, the brain still "remembers" how good hearing sounded and allows the hearing impaired to recover the lost ability relatively quickly. On the physiological level, "brain remembering how to hear" means that the brain cells responsible for processing audio information are still intact. The

5 Ching et al., 2001.

6 Abrahamson, 1997.

human brain has a unique ability to apply the brain cells not used for their original purpose to other tasks. Thus, in case of unaided hearing loss, the brain redistributes cells responsible for hearing to other functions. Once hearing loss becomes aided, it takes the brain approximately the same amount of time to return the brain cells back to hearing sense as it took to deploy them to other functions.

Both a person with sudden adult-onset hearing loss and a person with history of using hearing aids still have the hearing brain cells available for processing audio information. In these instances, aural rehabilitation after fitting with a hearing instrument is either unnecessary or short in time.

Let us take a closer look at people who lost their hearing at birth or early in their childhood. Speech is mostly developed during the first four years of life.[7] This means that people, who had lost their ability to hear before they reached the age of four, and did not use hearing instruments or implants, will not have the skills necessary to develop their speech even if aided later on. These people learn to communicate with each other using such means as sign language. Hearing instruments or implants will not help them to integrate into the hearing society. They could give these people only one benefit - the safety improvement due to increased awareness of environmental sounds such as an approaching car.

The third reason behind the lack of interest in social inclusion with the help of aided hearing is the reluctance of the hearing impaired who have been excluded from the hearing society to change their present lifestyle. Most often, this is the case with senior citizens, people older than 70-80 years, who spend almost all their time at home. When sensorineural hearing loss gradually develops, if left unaided, the hearing impaired gradually exclude themselves from the society. This usually happens due to inability to communicate successfully with other people. The hearing impaired gradually experience more difficulty in speech understanding during social gathering, group conversation, conversations held in noisy environment etc. Mental health problem such as depression, paranoia, fatigue etc begin to develop.[8] The hearing impaired start leading a rather secluded life, and steadily separate from the rest of the hearing society. They lose self-confidence and feel inadequate. As a result, they have no desire to return to the social life they led before hearing loss. Such cases are difficult to handle by an audiologist alone. A psychological help should be offered to go along with aided hearing.

The main reason for the lack of interest in social inclusion into the hearing society with the help of implants is prejudice against them. Numerous health economics studies show quality of life increase for the hearing impaired with

7 Reiter et al., 2012.

8 Kochkin & Rogin, 2000.

high degree of hearing loss after implantation compared to the situation before.[9] Nevertheless, for different reasons some deaf and hard of hearing are dead set against implantation. However, they have no objections to hearing aids. One reason is that they view their hearing loss not in terms of the hearing loss model, but in terms of the social model. A lot of them are people with severe to profound hearing loss, often deaf. They usually see themselves as a part of a distinct deaf culture, similar to how a person might feel a part of the ethnic, religious or musical culture. The very notion of treating their hearing loss with a cochlear implant may seem insulting to them. Besides, there are risks and disadvantages of the surgical procedure to install a cochlear implant. Cochlear is a very small and delicate part of the human body. Surgery is done in the area immediately adjacent to the nerve responsible for facial movements. Surgical mistakes could lead to severe complications. Some of the mistakes could result in temporary or permanent facial paralysis. In addition, a patient might experience temporary or permanent pain. There is the evidence that suggests this pain even led people to commit suicide. Moreover, in case of a traditional cochlear implant, all remaining hearing would be lost as a result of a surgery. For the deaf with some remaining hearing this is a significant argument against cochlear implantation. After the implantation, they will not have the ability to hear natural sounds at all. In the past years, electro-acoustic simulation implants were developed to address this particular concern. Recent advances in surgical methods made cochlear implantation safer than before. Nevertheless, the social model view risks remain unsolved.

Our first finding is that a hearing impaired person has to be willing to integrate into the normal-hearing society with the help of a hearing instrument or an implant in order to ensure the continuous use of aided hearing and social inclusion. It is consistent with the following discovery of Dillon (2001):

> "Initial motivation to obtain hearing aids has been shown to be a key determinant of whether patients continue to use hearing aids. A patient's motivation reflects the balance of all the advantages a patient expects hearing aids will provide offset by all the expected disadvantages, irrespective of whether all these positive and negative expectations are realistic."[10]

Other researchers also support our finding.[11]

---

[9] Cheng & Niparko, 1999; Wong et al., 2000; Niparko, 2009; Ruben, 2001; Joore et al., 2003; Keren at al., 2002; Mohr et al., 2000.

[10] Dillon, 2001, p. 209.

[11] Brooks, 1990; Erdman et al., 1984; Gatehouse, 1999; Hickson et al., 1986; and Hickson et al., 1999.

Another conclusion of the qualitative research is that the hearing loss measured objectively in dB is a poor predictor of the willingness to integrate into the normal-hearing society with the help of a hearing instrument or an implant. Similar findings can be found in the work of Dillon (2001). Dillon (2001) also notes that pure tone hearing loss

> "... is unreliable as a sole indicator of who will benefit from hearing aids, except in cases of normal hearing (no benefit) and severe hearing loss (substantial benefit)."[12]

We have discussed so far the reasons behind unwillingness of the hearing impaired to get a hearing instrument or an implant. Now, let us look at a situation when a person has no reservations about using a hearing instrument or an implant to integrate into the hearing society. In this case, we may assume that the person has definite skills and knowledge that allow her/him to be economically better off or have higher quality of life with aided hearing than with unaided hearing loss. But what if in reality it is not the case? If the perceived advantages of aided hearing are absent, a hearing impaired person does not have an important incentive for social integration with the help of a hearing instrument or an implant. People without such incentives are less likely to succeed in social integration. The question is how to differentiate between these people? Possible indicators for identifying skills or knowledge could be educational achievements and income. The problem with those is that many skills can be acquired outside the traditional education system via trainings, self-education, hands-on experience etc. Besides, in Russia and Ukraine there is a big difference in income level even among people with the same education. Their income often depends on the location within the country or even within the city. In economically more developed areas, a person receives a significantly higher pay than in less developed parts of the country for the same job. On top of everything, the hearing impaired can receive income from sources not directly related to their skills or knowledge level. These sources are money from leasing an asset, financial support from relatives, windfall gain etc.

Considering all above, what should we take as a reliable indicator to differentiate between the hearing impaired? During my qualitative research, I concluded that the communication needs of the hearing impaired could serve as an indicator. If skills or knowledge of the hearing impaired does not require communication ability to be properly utilized, then the hearing impaired, most likely, will not benefit that much from aided hearing. The hearing impaired who need to apply their communication skills daily will win the most. To determine

12 Dillon, 2001, p. 215.

at what degree the hearing impaired communicate in their everyday life, the following key needs were identified:

- The need to communicate over the phone;
- The need to lead a difficult conversation, such as
  a) conversation with a group of people;
  b) conversation in situations with loud background noise;
- The need to speak often with new people or strangers.

During the grounded theory building of my qualitative research, I concluded that the presence of these needs serves as a sufficient indicator for willingness to integrate into the hearing society with the help of a hearing instrument or an implant. The opposite is also true – if the hearing impaired do not have these needs, they will be less willing to become a part of the hearing society. The main advantage of using these needs as an indicator is that it is easy to question people about them and easy to verify if the answers are truthful.

These findings are also consistent with Dillon (2001)'s discovery:

> "… the more a person is in contact with other people (or would like to be if poor hearing was not a disincentive) the more likely it is that the advantages of hearing aids will outweigh their disadvantages. A hermit with a loud TV set and radio will not need hearing aids!"[13]

On the other hand, Dillon (2001) states that hearing aids are most helpful "in places that are quiet, and where speech is at a soft level."[14] Another extreme is that "if the primary need is to hear better in very noisy places, hearing aids may disappoint, irrespective of the degree of the patient's hearing loss."[15] At first glance, it may look like a contradiction to one of our qualitative research findings: people, who need to speak in a noisy environment will benefit from the hearing aids. Actually, it is not for the following reasons. First, since the time Dillon (2001) was published, hearing aids improved significantly in suppressing background noise. Besides, nowadays the majority of the hearing aids come with directional microphones that greatly improve speech understanding in a noisy environment. In addition, in one-on-one conversations in a quiet environment the hearing impaired may actually do well even without hearing aids as the speech understanding is better, and the use of other cues such as lip reading and gestures is easier.

---

13 Dillon, 2001, p. 219.

14 Dillon, 2001, p. 217.

15 Dillon, 2001, p. 217.

Social inclusion of the hearing impaired starts with the hearing aids purchase. Three main options are usually available to finance the hearing instruments and implants:

- buying with their own money and/or using reimbursement funds
- taking a loan to increase the amount of funds available for the purchase
- saving money to buy later

The hearing impaired can use either their money or different financial instruments to finance the purchase. Some of them can get money from standard bank savings accounts, consumer loans, collateralized loans, payday loans, rent-to-own agreements, hire purchase, pawnshops etc. Others use a combination of sources to access the funds. There are also those who decide to rent or lease a hearing aid.

During my research trip to Ukraine, I conducted an interview with the head of the organizational department of Ukrainian Deaf Society, Irina S.. In the course of our discussion, I have learned that in Ukraine, every 5 years, the hearing impaired with more than 75 dB hearing loss in both ears are eligible for a pair of free of charge hearing instruments from the government. In the year 2010, 282 people with severe hearing loss received such devices. Mostly, they were given very basic cheap analog instruments. The same year, the Ukranian government started offering digital trimmer devices, sadly only basic ones. Since the hearing impaired with less than 75 dB of hearing loss in any of the ears are not qualified to receive government help, and those who are qualified can get only poor quality hearing instruments, many hearing impaired are left to deal with their hearing loss on their own.

If a person has a profound hearing loss or even deafness in both ears, the Ukrainian government pays for one cochlear implant. In the year 2010, the official queue of the hearing impaired who wanted to get a free implant was 400 people. Unfortunately, only two people each year receive the implants from the government free of charge. At this rate, every new person with profound hearing loss in need of an implant should expect to wait around 200 years to get a free one!

From February 1, 2011, in Russia, the hearing impaired have the right for partial lump-sum reimbursement of the costs related to the purchase of hearing aids.[16] The size of the reimbursement varies depending on age of the hearing impaired, the region of residence, and the hearing loss in each ear.

During my interviews with the hearing impaired in Russia, I have discovered that many of them received reimbursement from the government in the

16 Ministry of Health Care and Social Development of Russian Federation, 2011.

range of 150-200 USD for hearing aid purchase per piece. This sum is sufficient to buy a very basic digital trimmer hearing instrument, but not enough to buy a computer-programmed digital hearing instrument. It is worth mentioning, for children the hearing instruments were often reimbursed completely.

Let us take a closer look at borrowing. During the qualitative research, I have found out that many hearing impaired are afraid of taking a loan – formal or informal. They often stated that they were worried a loan would impose an unbearable burden on their existing income level.

In the middle of my research trip to Ukraine, I had a discussion with a hearing impaired woman Olga. I met her at the Ukrainian Society of Deaf. She is in her thirties, and has about 70 dB hearing loss in both ears. Several months prior our meeting, she had bought a new hearing instrument for one ear (Oticon Sumo DM) for 24.000 Ukrain Hryvnas, which is roughly equal to 2950 USD. On the second ear, Olga still wears a 15 years old analog instrument. She has suffered from hearing loss since she was a 3 years old. As Olga was growing up in both hearing and deaf environments, she is able to speak with normal hearing people and is proficient in sign language. Olga is confident in her ability to work just as good if not better than normal hearing people do. Nevertheless, she fears she will not be able to get a better job due to rejections experienced in the past. She names stigma against the hearing impairment as the main reason, why she has difficulty finding a well-paid job. Besides, Olga needs a new hearing instrument for the second ear but does not have money to buy one. At the same time, she does not want to take a consumer loan for the purchase, because she fears of not being able to make regular monthly payments.

One may think that aided hearing will help to increase a hearing impaired person's income and allow her/him to pay back the debt almost at once. In reality the rehabilitation period of the hearing impaired after the first fit is often a lengthy process that requires professional, community and family support. It is especially true for the hearing impaired who had unaided hearing loss for a long time. Therefore, even if the hearing impaired expect to improve their financial situation after aiding their hearing ability, it will take some time to do that. Abrams et al. (1992) observed in their study that if after hearing aid fitting, the hearing impaired take part in the aural rehabilitation program, a significant reduction in the degree of perceived hearing handicap can be achieved.

To assess the borrowing capacity of the hearing impaired, we have to evaluate their willingness and ability to borrow money to finance a hearing instrument or an implant from formal and/or informal sources. Another important consideration is money availability to pay off the debt. The hearing impaired should have enough funds to make a living and regular loan payments. The rational hearing impaired will not take a loan to buy hearing instruments or implants if they know they will not be able to make monthly payments out of their current income.

Besides, individual borrowing in many developing countries requires collateral. Therefore, readiness to take a loan also depends on the availability of assets.

Now, let us take a look at the situation when a hearing impaired person has the willingness to hear better and the ability to borrow money. Her/his current income level allows making regular loan payments. So far, this sounds good from the financial point of view: if a loan is taken, it can be paid back. However, this person might still decide against the loan if her/his previous experience with hearing instruments was bad. In this case, she/he might not see the investment in aided hearing as meaningful. On the other hand, if the person does have positive experience with hearing instruments, she/he will be more willing to borrow in order to upgrade existing or buy new hearing aids and take advantage of the latest speech understanding technologies. The new technologies help to improve everyday communication remarkably.

If a hearing impaired person has never had a hearing aid, there is a high possibility that she/he did not use her/his hearing ability properly for a long time. In such a case, we, most likely, should expect a slow recovery and significant time for rehabilitation. Based on my qualitative research, I would not recommend adding a burden of interest and principal payment on the hearing impaired in this situation.

The main conditions for a hearing impaired person to take a loan for a hearing instrument or an implant purchase are the following:

- she/he has already had some positive experience with aided hearing
- she/he is willing to borrow
- she/he has necessary assets to use as collateral

The more terms are met, the higher the probability that the hearing impaired will take a loan.

Now, let us look into savings for a hearing instrument or an implant purchase. The amount of savings depends on the income and consumption level of the hearing impaired and/or their immediate family members. The time value of money and propensity to save also influence the savings sum. Government reimbursement programs and health insurance coverage determine the need to save. If the hearing impaired do not qualify for these programs, they have to put away more money or look for other solutions to get hearing aids. In many developing countries and the USA, reimbursements are normally available for people with profound hearing loss and deafness. In cases of less severe hearing loss, the hearing impaired usually rely on savings and other financial tools.

To summarize, a hearing impaired person will consider saving and/or using currently available external funds for a purchase of a hearing instrument or an implant if:

- she/he has enough income left after deducting taxes and living expenses to make savings
- she/he is qualified for external help
- she/he has a personal discount rate for the time value of money significantly higher than 0

The more terms are met, the higher the probability that the hearing impaired will benefit from saving for a hearing instrument or an implant purchase.

5 Quantitative Research on the Healthcare Economic Policy for Hearing Impairment

5.1 Methodology and Research Design

The second part of the research on financing social inclusion of the hearing impaired is based on quantitative verification of the findings made in the first qualitative part of the research. The data for the verification was collected from a survey. The method used for quantitative verification of the qualitative research result is confirmatory factor analysis. This method is a type of structural equation modeling.[1] The idea behind this approach is that a researcher verifies if the model built by her/him fits the data collected to confirm the theoretical model. In our case, the model is developed based on qualitative research. Literature suggests that in many cases qualitative research helps to build apriori models.[2] Another possible approach to prepare the input is theoretical model building. However, it is not relevant to this study.

In qualitative research, we have identified two most important factors behind the successful social inclusion of the hearing impaired through financing their hearing instruments or implants. They are:

- willingness to integrate into the hearing society with the help of hearing aids
- depending on personal situation, willingness and ability to borrow and/or save to finance a hearing instrument or an implant

The second factor is actually a combination of saving and borrowing sub-factors. These are latent variables, they cannot be observed directly. Still, we can study them researching survey indicators. Several indicators grouped together form a latent variable.

The latent variables for this research were determined to be:

- Willingness to integrate into the hearing society
- Willingness and ability to borrow
- Willingness and ability to save

In total, there are 9 observed variables that predict these 3 variables.

---

1 Kline, 2011.

2 Preedy & Watson, 2009.

For "Willingness to integrate into the hearing society", we use the following observed variables:

1) The need to communicate over the phone
2) The need to lead difficult conversations, such as
   - Group conversation
   - Conversation with loud background noise
3) The need to speak often with new people, strangers

For "Willingness and ability to borrow", the observed variables are:

4) Positive experience with aided hearing
5) Willingness and ability to take a loan (formal or informal)
6) Availability of the necessary assets to put as collateral if needed

For "Willingness and ability to save", they are:

7) Sufficient income left after deducting living expenses and taxes
8) Access to partial or full reimbursement
9) Personal discount rate for time value of money

The survey questions are built to allow getting direct information about the indicators. The collected information is analyzed in AMOS 20.0 – a statistical package for structural equation modeling developed by IBM SPSS.

5.2 Research Setting and Data Collection

The survey data is collected using SurveyMonkey – an online survey tool. The survey was conducted from March 4, 2012 to October 31, 2012. It was created in 2 languages – Russian and English. Total 250 responses were received, out of them 190 are in Russian language and 60 in English. 128 Russian and 53 English answers were complete. The majority of the responses in the English language survey were from the USA. Some were from Canada, Czech Republic, Germany, New Zealand, India, Australia, Hungary, Bangladesh, South Africa, Netherlands, Philippines, and Israel. The most answers in Russian language were from Russia and Ukraine. Some of the responses were from Moldova, Kazakhstan, Belarus, and Estonia.

The survey participants were recruited via social media such as Facebook and different forums for the hearing impaired. Due to my 12 years of experience in the hearing instruments industry, I could discuss hearing loss related topics with the hearing impaired freely. My answers to their questions were credible and helped me to gain their trust. As a result, they were willing to fill out the survey.

Out of 181 survey participants, who completed the survey, 147 indicated that they had aided hearing experience at one point of their life, while 34 have never had neither a hearing instrument nor an implant. Out of 147 respondents with aided hearing experience, 135 stated that they use either a hearing instrument or an implant in their daily life.

In this research we use a weighted least squares (WLS) estimator to perform confirmatory factor analysis (CFA). The sample size is a very important consideration to carry out robust CFA.[3] He suggested that for the weighted least squares estimation method, the optimal ratio of cases (completed surveys) to the number of model parameters (indicators) should be between 10 and 20. Kline (2011) also indicated the absolute minimum value of such ratio. If a model has observed variables, then the sample size shall exceed

$$n(n+1)/2+n \quad (1)$$

In our model, n equals 9 as we have nine observed variables. Therefore, the optimal amount of completed surveys shall be between 100 and 200, but no less than

$$n(n+1)/2+n=9(9+1)/2+9=54 \quad (2)$$

For this research, 181 survey participants completed the survey. This number gives us confidence that the sample size is sufficient to execute confirmatory factor analysis successfully.

5.3 Survey Design

The survey is designed to cover multiple aspects of hearing loss and preferences of the hearing impaired in order to find the optimal way for financing their social inclusion.

First, the survey collects the information on hearing loss of a participant. The same set of questions about hearing loss is asked for the right ear, and for the left one. The following topics are covered in the first part of the survey:

- Subjective hearing loss: hearing impaired self-perception of hearing loss

3 Kline, 2011.

- Objective hearing loss: air conduction audiogram
- Type of the hearing instrument or the implant used
- Channel through which the hearing aid was purchased
- Technology used in the hearing aid (digital or analog)
- Satisfaction level with the hearing aid
- Model and manufacturer of the hearing aid
- How long this particular hearing aid is used
- Prior experience with aided hearing

As a next step, the demographic information about the hearing impaired is collected, including:

- Time of hearing loss occurrence
- Time needed to get back to work after getting first hearing aids (effective rehabilitation period length)
- Age
- Gender
- Education level
- Employment status
- Size of the settlement, where a hearing impaired person lives
- Country of residence
- Marital status

Next, work activity is covered:

- Professional occupation
- Physical activities
- PC usage at work
- The need to communicate over the phone
- The need to speak one-on-one with others in a quiet environment
- The need to lead a difficult conversation, such as
  a) Conversation with a group of people
  b) Conversation in situations with background noise

- The need to speak often with new people, strangers
- Household income level
- Household size

Later, we adjust the household income to account for differences in cost of living between areas where the hearing impaired live and differences in household size.

The questions that cover work activity help to obtain the information necessary to validate the factor of willingness to integrate into the hearing society with the help of hearing instruments and implants.

Next, we gather data on hearing health utility of the hearing impaired. The hearing impaired with prior aided experience answer how the hearing aids help them in their daily activities. In other words, we obtain hearing health utility information after fitting with hearing instruments or implants. Please note that this information is relevant only to the hearing impaired, who have prior experience with hearing aids. The hearing impaired without such experience cannot give any meaningful information. Therefore, to assess their hearing health utility, we ask different questions. Namely, we use the questions on Time-trade-off and Standard Gamble measurements. We will review them in more detail later.

To collect data about the hearing impaired with prior aided experience, we use both International Outcome Inventory for Hearing Aids (IOI-HA) and Satisfaction in Amplification in Daily Life (SADL) questionnaires. They measure subjective benefits of aided hearing. The International Outcome Inventory for Hearing Aids is the questionnaire for self-report of outcome measures for the hearing impaired with hearing aids. Cox et al. (2000) recommend it to help researchers make their inquiry on hearing loss comparable.

Objective benefits of hearing aids lie outside the scope of this research. For social inclusion of the hearing impaired, our goal is not to establish the audibility from technological point of view, but to identify ways in which hearing impaired can be better included in the hearing world. As subjective benefits of hearing aids cover not only technological aspects of sound amplification, but also such elements as rehabilitation, counseling and fine-tuning, they fit our purpose.

International Outcome Inventory for Hearing Aids is a short questionnaire consisting of 7 questions.[4] It allows to measure health outcomes of fitting with a hearing aid along with the dimensions of Introspection and Interaction.[5] IOI-HA is intended to be a supplement for other outcome schemes.[6]

---

4 Cox et al., 2000.

5 Cox & Alexander, 2002.

6 Cox et al., 2000.

The questions are the following:

1. Think about how much you used your present hearing aid(s) over the past two weeks. On an average day, how many hours did you use the hearing aid(s)?
   a. None
   b. Less than 1 hour a day
   c. 1 to 4 hours a day
   d. 4 to 8 hours a day
   e. More than 8 hours a day
2. Think about the situation where you most wanted to hear better, before you got your present hearing aid(s). Over the past two weeks, how much has the hearing aid helped in that situation?
   a. Helped not at all
   b. Helped slightly
   c. Helped moderately
   d. Helped quite a lot
   e. Helped very much
3. Think again about the situation where you most wanted to hear better. When you use your present hearing aid(s), how much difficulty do you STILL have in that situation?
   a. Very much difficulty
   b. Quite a lot of difficulty
   c. Moderate difficulty
   d. Slight difficulty
   e. No difficulty
4. Considering everything, do you think your present hearing aid(s) is worth the trouble?
   a. Not at all worth it
   b. Slightly worth it
   c. Moderately worth it
   d. Quite a lot worth it
   e. Very much worth it

5. Over the past two weeks, with your present hearing aid(s), how much have your hearing difficulties affected the things you can do?

   a. Affected very much
   b. Affected quite a lot
   c. Affected moderately
   d. Affected slightly
   e. Affected not at all

6. Over the past two weeks, with your present hearing aid(s), how much do you think other people were bothered by your hearing difficulties?

   a. Bothered very much
   b. Bothered quite a lot
   c. Bothered moderately
   d. Bothered slightly
   e. Bothered not at all

7. Considering everything, how much has your present hearing aid(s) changed your enjoyment of life?

   a. Worse
   b. No change
   c. Slightly better
   d. Quite a lot better
   e. Very much better

Another important questionnaire used in our survey is Satisfaction in Amplification in Daily Life (SADL). This questionnaire allows to measure health outcome along the dimensions of Positive Effect, Service & Cost, Negative Features, and Personal Image.[7]

For all questions in the SADL Questionnaire the following answers are possible:

a. Not at all
b. A little
c. Somewhat

7 Cox & Alexander, 1999.

d. Medium
e. Considerably
f. Greatly
g. Tremendously

The questions are the following:

1. Compared to using no hearing aids at all, do your hearing aids help you understand people you speak with most frequently?
2. Are you *frustrated* when your hearing aids pick up sounds that keep you from hearing what you want to hear?
3. Are you convinced that obtaining your hearing aids was in your best Interests?
4. Do you think people notice your hearing loss more when you wear your hearing aids?
5. Do your hearing aids reduce the number of times you have to ask people to repeat?
6. Do you think your hearing aids are worth the trouble?
7. Are you bothered by an inability to get enough loudness from your hearing aids without feedback (whistling)?
8. How content are you with the appearance of your hearing aids?
9. Does wearing your hearing aids improve your self-confidence?
10. How natural is the sound from your hearing aids?
11. How helpful are your hearing aids on MOST telephones with NO amplifier or loudspeaker?
12. How competent was the person who provided you with your hearing aids?
13. Do you think wearing your hearing aids makes you seem less capable?
14. Does the cost of your hearing aids seem reasonable to you?
15. How pleased are you with the dependability (how often they need repairs) of your hearing aids?

Both IOI-HA and SADL are integrated in the survey.

In order to calculate health utility of the hearing impaired who had neither hearing instruments nor implants we use the following approaches:

- Time-trade-off (TTO), and
- Standard Gamble (SG).

They are standard health-economics tools used in various health economic studies.[8] Time-trade-off and Standard Gamble are not specific for hearing loss health outcomes measurements. Time-trade-off method measures preferences under certainty. On the contrary, Standard Gamble measures preferences under uncertainty.

In order to estimate health utility for the unaided hearing impaired under certainty (TTO) the following question is asked:

> Imagine a situation: you live the next 10 years with your current hearing loss but without the help of hearing aids. Now concentrate and try to estimate how many years of life with 100% hearing you consider equivalent to those 10 years.

In order to estimate health utility for the unaided hearing impaired under uncertainty (SG) the following question is asked:

> Imagine a pure hypothetical situation: you come to see your doctor. To your surprise, she has some interesting news for you. The doctor tells you that you have a unique type of hearing loss and there are no existing hearing aids that you could use to help you hear better. Besides, untreated, this hearing loss will lead you to death in around 10 years. But there is hope. They have an experimental free of charge treatment that, if successful, completely restores the hearing. The bad news is that in some cases it has severe side effects, even death can occur.
>
> Thus, you have only two options:
>
> 1. Reject the free of charge treatment course, and live another 10 years without hearing aids.
>
> 2. Take part in the treatment, which will either restore your hearing completely or make some major damage to your health including death.
>
> Knowing all of the above, indicate the MINIMAL success rate of the treatment, which will make you consider taking a risk and undergoing the treatment.

During the qualitative research phase, it was identified that prior positive experience with aided hearing is an important component of readiness to take a loan for purchase of a hearing instrument or an implant. On the other hand, lack of such experience will be a strong argument for the hearing impaired against borrowing. We are able to verify this finding using self-assessment of health utility.

Next, we need to confirm the willingness to borrow. Many people are ready to ask for a loan only from certain types of lenders, while unwilling to borrow from others. Therefore, in the survey we ask about the willingness to borrow from formal institutions (banks, credit unions, hearing instrument dispenser etc.) and informal sources (relatives, friends, family, neighbors).

---

8 Burstrom et al., 2006; Dolan et al., 1996a; Dolan et al., 1996b; Martin et al., 2000; and Gold et al., 1996.

The last piece of information missing to verify the qualitative research finding on borrowing willingness is the readiness to sell assets or use them as collateral. It was assessed by asking the following question:

What would you recommend your friend, who has the same hearing loss like you do, but cannot afford to buy hearing aids right now? Select everything that applies

- To take a loan in a bank, credit union or in another credit organization
- To borrow the money from friends, family or relatives
- To save the money for the purchase on a bank account
- To save the money in cash (at home or in the other place, but not in a bank, credit union or another credit organization)
- To sell some of his belongings, appliances or property in order to get the money to buy the hearing aid(s)
- To buy the hearing aids that he can afford right now without any loans
- Not to buy hearing aids at all, because they don't help
- Not to buy hearing aids at all, because you know how to get them for free (government program etc.)

The last component of financing a hearing instrument or an implant purchase is saving. The income adjusted by cost of living and household size was calculated. The question on preferences of the hearing impaired regarding a certain sum of money today versus the same amount of money in one month and similar questions helped to determine the personal discount rate for the time value of money. Analyzing the answer, we are able to understand the "near term" and "distant" choices of the hearing impaired. Hyperbolic preferences manifest themselves in the choice of immediate reward in the near term along with the choice of delayed reward in the long term. Consistent impatience is seen in selecting immediate reward both in the near term and in distant cases, while consistent patience is seen in choosing delayed reward both in the near term and in the long term. Seemingly illogical choice of being patient now, but impatient later can be explained with the presence of cash now, but foreseeing that it might disappear in the future. Ashraf et al. (2006) use this approach for assessing personal discount rates for the time value of money. They find no gender difference, although married women are more impatient than unmarried. Moreover, education is uncorrelated with impatience; unemployed individuals are more impatient, and higher income households are more patient. Saving requires a delay of immediate rewards for greater future benefits and thus is considered particularly difficult for individuals who have hyperbolic preferences or self-control problems.[9] Therefore, for such people commitment saving products are recommended. In our case, we consider the hearing inpaired with consistent impatience as having the highest discount rate followed by seemingly illogical (patient now, impatient later) hearing inpaired. Next come the hearing impaired with hyperbolic preferences. And last, people with consistent patience are seen as the best savers.

The last component of savings factor is reimbursement funds available for the hearing impaired. These funds can come from various sources such as government, insurance and charity organisations. Each of these institutions can provide partial or complete reimbursement. The data on reimbursement was collected and later aggregated to get a consolidated picture on the reimbursement level for every survey participant.

5.4 Processing Survey Results

5.4.1 Observed Variables for "Willingness to integrate into the hearing society"

During the qualitative research phase, the communication needs were identified as sufficient indicators of willingness to integrate into the hearing society with the help of a hearing instrument or an implant. They are the three first observed variables mentioned above:

- The need to communicate over the phone;
- The need to lead a difficult conversation, such as
  a) Conversation with a group of people;
  b) Conversation in situations with loud background noise;
- The need to speak often with new people and strangers.

Using confirmatory factor analysis, we assigned a variable for each of these needs and named it accordingly: the variable "*phone_use*" for the first need, the variable "*dif.Conver*" (meaning difficult conversations) for the second one, and the variable "*strangers*" for the third. These variables together form a factor we called "Willingness to integrate into the hearing society". In the survey, the hearing impaired were asked to choose between two statements:

- I speak a lot over the phone
- I rarely speak over the phone

---

9 Ashraf et al., 2006.

If a hearing impaired person chooses the first statement, then the variable "*phone_use*" is given the value "1". If she/he selects the second answer, it is assigned the value "0". We use the variable "*phone_use*" later in confirmatory factor analysis as an observed variable associate with the factor "Willingness to integrate into the hearing society".

In the survey, we also asked the hearing impaired to place a mark next to all of the three statements that are true for them:

- I often speak in groups
- I often have to speak in situations with a lot of background noise
- I rarely need to speak at my work

If any or the first two statements are checked, then the variable "*dif.Conver*" gets the value "1" assigned. If none of the first two answers is selected, but the third one is, "*dif.Conver*" is given the value "0". We later utilize this variable in confirmatory factor analysis as an observed variable associated with the factor "Willingness to integrate into the hearing society".

Additionally, we ask the survey participants to choose between two statements:

- I have to speak often with new people
- Mostly, I speak only with people whom I know very well

If a person with hearing loss checks the first option, the variable "*strangers*" is assigned the value "1". If she/he selects the second answer, "strangers" is given the value "0". The variable "*strangers*" is also used later in confirmatory factor analysis as a predictor of the factor "Willingness to integrate into the hearing society".

5.4.2 Observed Variables for "Willingness and ability to borrow"

During the qualitative research phase, the following components were identified as sufficient indicators of willingness and ability to borrow for the purchase of a hearing instrument or an implant:

- A hearing impaired person has already had some positive experience with aided hearing;
- A hearing impaired person is willing and able to take a loan (formal or informal);
- A hearing impaired person has necessary assets and is willing to use them as collateral if needed.

To assess prior experience with aided hearing, we apply the standard International Outcome Inventory for Hearing Aids (IOI-HA) and Satisfaction in Amplification in Daily Life (SADL) questionnaires discussed earlier. Both are self-report outcome assessments. The goal of these questionnaires is to evaluate the degree at which provision of hearing instruments or implants helps individual patients overcome their hearing difficulties. Self-reporting schemes used in this research address questions about personal image, negative features, service costs, positive effect, quality of life, impact on others, satisfaction with amplification, and residual activity limitation.

In case of the IOI-HA questionnaire, we calculate the average of all seven answers to produce the IOI-HA score for every survey participant. As we know, every single IOI-HA question has five possible answers. These answers are lined up in order of increasing satisfaction with aided hearing. The average of them is also aligned accordingly. Correspondingly, the maximal possible value of the average is five – the highest level of satisfaction with aided hearing. The minimal value is one – the lowest satisfaction with hearing aids. In this research, we uniformize the obtained IOI-HA score to make it a value between zero and one. This value is the quality of life measure as per IOI-HA questionnaire.

Similarly, we assess the quality of life with the help of Satisfaction in Amplification in Daily Life questionnaire. Having calculated the SADL score, we also uniformize it to be a value between zero and one.

Since the IOI-HA and the SADL questionnaires measure the same underlying concept – satisfaction with aided hearing, the values of the SADL score and the IOI-HA score shall not differ much from each other. Indeed, this is what we see looking at the results (Table 2) derived from our survey. Correlation between two scores is significant.

Next, we find the average of the uniformized IOI-HA and SADL quality of life estimates. It is the average value of quality of life for aided hearing impaired. For our further research, we name this value "*AposterioriQALY_uniform*". It shows the overall satisfaction with aided hearing.

In the survey, we also assess the willingness and ability to take a formal (via bank or other institution) or informal (via family and friends) loan. For both cases, the following options to choose from were available:

- I would never take a loan
- I would like to take a loan, but unable to do so
- I would borrow up to 10% of the cost of hearing aids
- I would borrow up to 30% of the cost of hearing aids
- I would borrow up to 50% of the cost of hearing aids
- I would borrow up to 70% of the cost of hearing aids
- I would borrow up to 100% of the cost of hearing aids

Table 2: SADL score and IOI-HA score.[10]

Descriptive Statistics

	Mean	Std. Deviation	N
IOIHAscore	,366	,1602	181
SADLscore	,5010602473	,2020944451	181

Correlations

		IOIHAscore	SADLscore
IOIHAscore	Pearson Correlation	1	,813**
	Sig. (2-tailed)		,000
	N	181	181
SADLscore	Pearson Correlation	,813**	1
	Sig. (2-tailed)	,000	
	N	181	181

**. Correlation is significant at the 0.01 level (2-tailed).

To calculate the value of this observed variable, the maximum value between the values of two choices (a value of willingness and ability to take a formal loan, a value of willingness and ability to take an informal loan) was used. The resulting value was also uniformized to vary from 0 to 1. Here, 0 corresponds to absolute unwillingness to take a loan, and 1 matches the willingness and ability to finance 100% of the hearing aids cost with the help of a loan. For further research, we named this indicator "*borrow_uniform*".

To assess the presence of collateral, we asked the hearing impaired if they would recommend a friend with the same hearing loss to sell some of her/his belongings, appliances or assets to get money to buy hearing aid(s). The use of this indirect question helped us to evaluate the hearing impaireds' attitude on the subject without such objections as:

- My bank can give me a loan even without collateral;
- I have enough money, so I don't need a loan right now;
- I have a hearing instrument right now, so I don't need to put up collateral to take a loan to buy a new one.

10 Own illustration using IBM SPSS 19.0.

Besides, inquiring about a friend with the same hearing loss simplifies the question for the hearing impaired. They do not get distracted with their personal situation. Their reaction only indicates the willingness to put up collateral. There are only two possible answers to the question – yes or no. The hearing impaired who answered "no" correspond to the value 0 in their willingness to put up collateral, those who said "yes" correspond to the value 1. To use later, we named this indicator "*sell_assets*".

5.4.3 Observed Variables for "Willingness and ability to save"

During the qualitative research phase, the following components were identified as sufficient indicators of willingness and ability to save or use currently available funds for a hearing instrument or an implant purchase:

- A hearing impaired person has some income left after deducting taxes and living expenses to make savings;
- A hearing impaired person has access to partial or full reimbursement;
- A hearing impaired person has a personal discount rate for time value of money, which is significantly higher than 0.

The survey includes the question on the total monthly household income to evaluate income level of the hearing impaired. Survey participants had to choose between 10 income levels:

- less than 99 US Dollars
- from 100 to 299 US Dollars
- from 300 to 599 US Dollars
- from 600 to 999 US Dollars
- from 1000 to 1499 US Dollars
- from 1500 to 1999 US Dollars
- from 2000 to 2999 US Dollars
- from 3000 to 3999 US Dollars
- from 4000 to 4999 US Dollars
- more than 5000 US Dollars

In addition, the survey contains the questions about:

- country of residence of the hearing impaired;
- size of the human settlement where the hearing impaired live;
- household size of the hearing impaired.

Based on this information, we adjusted[11] the income level to account for differences in cost of living between various countries, larger cities versus smaller towns, and different family sizes. The resulting income level was uniformized to a value between 0 and 1. Here, 0 corresponds to the income level, when a hearing impaired person has absolutely nothing left after buying food and other basic necessities. On the other hand, 1 matches the income level of an affluent hearing impaired person who is able to afford a pair of high-end hearing instruments within one monthly income. We named this indicator *"monthly_income_uniform"*.

To evaluate if the hearing impaired qualify for external help, the following three questions were offered:

- Indicate at what degree your health insurance covers the cost of your hearing aids
- Indicate at what degree the government covers the cost of your hearing aids
- Indicate at what degree the charity help covers the cost of your hearing aids

To quantify the access to reimbursement, we took the maximum value between all three (health insurance, government, and charity). The resulting value was uniformized to vary from 0 to 1. The value 0 is given when a hearing impaired person has absolutely no access to reimbursement. The value 1 corresponds with 100% reimbursement of the hearing aids costs. We called this indicator "*reimbursement_uniform*".

To evaluate the personal discount rate for the time value of money, we follow the approach proposed by Ashraf et al. (2006). The hearing impaired were asked if they would prefer to have a definite sum of money today or in one month. It helped to determine the "near term" frame. The same questions were asked again, but this time the choice was between receiving the money in 6 months or in 7. This way the "long term" frame was estimated. The hearing impaired, who constantly chose to get a higher reward later, can be described as "patient". Apparently their discount rate is quite low and consistent between the near- and the long-term. Those who chose an immediate reward in the near-term but decided to be patient in the long-term can be described as "hyperbolic". They have a bit higher discount rate, and their discount rate is inconsistent over time.

---

[11] For detailed description of the logic behind the income adjustment, please refer to the appendix A-2.

The hearing impaired who chose an immediate reward in the long-term but decided to be patient in the short-term can be identified as "patient now and impatient later". The explanation behind this is that they have money now but foresee liquidity constraints in 6 months. These people have even higher discount rate, although, like in previous case, it is inconsistent over time. The highest discount rate have individuals who are impatient both in the "near term" and in the "long term". To obtain a uniformized measure of the time value of money, we assigned the following values:

- 1 – a "patient" hearing impaired person;
- 0.66 – a "hyperbolic" hearing impaired person;
- 0.33 – a "patient now and impatient later" hearing impaired person;
- 0 – an "impatient" hearing impaired person.

We named this indicator "*time_preference_uniform*".

Now that we have identified all relevant variables for confirmatory factor analysis, our next step is to perform it to verify the results of the qualitative research. The overview of the latent and observed variables is shown in the Table 3.

Table 3: Overview of the latent and observed variables.

Latent variables	Observed variables
Willingness to integrate into the hearing society	The need to communicate over the phone
	The need to lead difficult conversations, such as group conversation and conversation with loud background noise
	The need to speak often with new people, strangers
Willingness and ability to borrow	Positive experience with aided hearing
	Willingness and ability to take a loan (formal or informal)
	Availability of the necessary assets to put as collateral if needed
Willingness and ability to save	Sufficient income left after deducting living expenses and taxes
	Access to partial or full reimbursement
	Personal discount rate for time value of money

5.5 Assumptions behind Confirmatory Factor Analysis

In CFA model, we test the hypothesis that the parameters of the measurement model, such as factor loadings and factor correlations, allow us to reproduce the observed covariances between the observed variables.[12]

The fundamental equation of the confirmatory factor analysis is the following:

$$y_j = \lambda_{j,1}\eta_1 + \lambda_{j,2}\eta_2 + \ldots + \lambda_{j,m}\eta_m + \varepsilon_j \qquad (3)$$

where

- y_j is the j-th observed variable (in our research, we have identified the following variables: "The need to communicate over the phone", "The need to lead difficult conversations, such as group conversation and conversation with loud background noise", "The need to speak often with new people, strangers", "Positive experience with aided hearing", "Willingness and ability to take a loan (formal or informal)", "Availability of the necessary assets to put as collateral if needed", "Sufficient income left after deducting living expenses and taxes", "Access to partial or full reimbursement", and "Personal discount rate for time value of money");
- $\lambda_{j,m}$ is the factor loading relating observed variable y_j to the m-th factor (or latent variable);
- $\eta_m$represents the m-th factor (in our case, these are the following latent vari ables or factors: "Willingness to integrate into the society with the help of a hearing instrument or an implant", "Willingness and ability to borrow", and "Willingness and ability to save");
- ε_j is the error residual associated with the observed variable y_j, which is independent of all other observed variables and their error residuals.

In confirmatory factor analysis, observed variables are thought to be caused by factors. The objective of CFA is to test whether the data fits the measurement model. The measurement model specifies the number of factors, how observed variables are related to these factors, and the relationship between error residuals associated with the observed variables. As we can see from the fundamental equation of the factor analysis (3), the first assumption of CFA is the linear relationship between factors and observed variables. Another assumption is that dimensionality (number of factors behind the observed variables) is known.

12 Jöreskog & Sörbom, 1996.

Moreover, it is understood that the error residual ε_j of each observed variable is independent after controlling for factors, unless otherwise explicitly stated in the model.

The most frequently used estimation method in CFA is maximum likelihood (ML). Using this or some other estimation method, we can statistically evaluate how close the covariances of the observed variables are to the predicted covariances of the observed variables that come from the statistical model. ML and other estimation methods produce various fit indices. These fit indices are used to assess the goodness of fit of the model. Basically, they tell us how far the predicted covariances are from the covariances we obtain from the survey data. When using the maximum likelihood method, we assume the normal distribution of the observed and latent variables. Another assumption behind ML is the large sample size. Unfortunately, this method requires input variables to be continous and multivariate normal, although minor departures from normality assumption are still tolerable for maximum likelihood method.[13] West et al. (1995) point to the following consequences if normality assumption is violated:

- Inflated χ^2 values;
- Underestimation of goodness of fit statistics, such as Tucker-Lewis Index (TLI) and Comparative Fit Index (CFI);
- Underestimation of standard errors of the parameter estimates, which can lead to the erroneous conclusion that the parameter is significantly different from 0 even if it is not the case.

In this research, many of the indicators (observed variables) used as input to the model are not only non-normal, but also categorical in nature. Brown (2006) points to the following consequences of treating categorical variables as continuous:

- Underestimation of correlations among indicators;
- Incorrect test statistics and standard errors;
- Incorrect parameter estimates.

Therefore, when input data have either pronounced skewness or kurtosis, or some of the input variables are not continous, maximum likelihood method cannot be used. There are various estimators available for categorical data, such as unweighted least squares, robust weighted least squares, weighted least squares

13 Chou & Bentler, 1995.

etc. The most frequently used estimator for categorical data is weighted least squares (WLS).[14]

In confirmatory factor analysis, the null hypothesis assumes that if the hypothesized model is correct, the sample variance-covariance matrix will be exactly reproduced by the estimated variance-covariance matrix that comes from the model. CFA calculation with weighted least squares estimator is an iterative procedure. It starts from the sample variance-covariance matrix. We use the symbol S to describe this matrix in our research. As we have 9 observed variables, it is a 9×9-matrix. The WLS method estimates the unknown variables of the model. In our case, unknown variables are factor loadings $\lambda_{j,m}$ and a variance-covariance matrix of latent variables. With the help of these estimates, the predicted variance-covariance matrix is calculated. In this research, the symbol Σ is used to describe this matrix. Again, it is a 9×9-matrix. The WLS method employs a weight matrix for residuals. To describe this matrix in our research, we use the symbol W. The matrix W is based on the estimates of variances and covariances of each element of the matrix S.[15] More specifically, the matrix W is calculated using the following equation[16]:

$$(N-1)W(s_{ij}, s_{gh}) = \sigma_{ig}\sigma_{jh} + \sigma_{jh}\sigma_{jg} \tag{4}$$

where

- $W(s_{ij}, s_{gh})$ represents the element of the matrix W describing the covariance between the estimates of the elements of matrix S: S_{ij} and S_{gh};
- σ_{ij} is the estimate of the covariance between i-th and j-th observed variable;
- N represents the number of distinct elements of the matrix S. In our case $N = 45$.

These "covariances of covariances" are related to kurtosis estimates. This means that the fit function of WLS is weighted by variances and kurtosis in order to compensate for violations of the normality assumption. Using the matrix W, WLS overrides violations of multivariate normality, which is a standard assumption for the maximum likelihood method.

The matrix W is typically quite large. In our research, we have 3 factors, each one has 3 observed variables. Therefore, we have 9 observed variables in total. All of them can make combinations of 2 with each other to produce covari-

14 Browne, 1984.

15 Kaplan, 2000.

16 Kaplan, 2000, p.82.

ances. In general, we know that if a set has n elements, then the number of subsets each containing k elements is

$$\binom{n}{k} = \frac{n!}{k!(n-k)!} \tag{5}$$

It is easy to compute that if $n = 9$, and $k = 2$, then the number of covariances is $9*8/2 = 36$.

Taking into consideration all said above, we also have 9 variances on the main diagonal of the matrix S. It means that we have in total 36 + 9 = 45 elements in the matrix S. It is easy to see that

$$n(n-1)/2 + n = n(n+1)/2 \tag{6}$$

Therefore, another way to compute the number of distinct elements of the matrix S is the following: $n(n+1)/2 = 9(9+1)/2 = 45$. The matrix W has the order 45 by 45 and contains 1035 distinct elements.[17]

The WLS fitting function is used to assess the difference between the observed and the predicted data. The WLS fitting function looks like this[18]:

$$F_{WLS} = (s-\sigma)'W^{-1}(s-\sigma) \tag{7}$$

where

- F_{WLS} is the fitting function, its value needs to be minimized;
- s and σ are the vectors that contain all the distinct elements of the matrices S and Σ respectively.

The WLS method works even without specifying a particular distribution for the observed variables. For that reason, another name used to discribe WLS estimator is asymptotic distribution free (ADF) function.[19]

After calculating the fitting function, the next iteration starts with refinement of the estimates for the unknown variables. Please refer to the section 5.6 for more details on the iterative refinement of the estimates used in the fitting function. As mentioned above, we apply a special computer program AMOS 20.0 to do that. It analyses data via structural equation modeling approach. With every iteration, the program reduces the value of F_{WLS}. When no further improvement of the matrix Σ is possible, the CFA algorithm finishes the work and

17 Calculated using the equation (6): 45*(45+1)/2=1035.
18 Browne, 1984.
19 Browne, 1984.

reports the best estimates it could find for the unknown variables along with various goodness-of-fit statistics.

In general, CFA can output either standardized or unstandardized solutions. Under a CFA solution we understand factor loadings and error residuals. An unstandardized solution is scale sensitive. Typically, it is used to compare solutions over time or across groups. In this case, a variance of the observed variable does not necessarily equals 1. To produce a standardized solution, an unstandardized solution is transformed to have the factor variance to be equal to 1. The relationship between the standardized and unstandardized factor loadings is the following[20]:

$$\lambda_{u(yx)} = (\lambda_{s(yx)} SD_y)/(SD_x) \tag{8}$$

where

- $\lambda_{u(yx)}$ – unstandardized factor loading of the observed variable y on the latent variable x;
- $\lambda_{s(yx)}$ – completely standardized factor loading of the observed variable y on the latent variable x;
- SD_y – standard deviation of the observed variable y;
- SD_x – standard deviation of the latent variable x.

The relationship between the standardized and unstandardized error residuals is the following[21]:

$$\varepsilon_{u(y)} = \varepsilon_{s(y)} \sigma_{yy}^2 \tag{9}$$

where

- $\varepsilon_{u(y)}$ – unstandardized error residual of an observed variable y;
- $\varepsilon_{s(y)}$ – standardized error residual of an observed variable y;
- σ_{yy}^2 – observed variance of an observed variable y.

Besides, latent variables should have their scale identified. In order to ensure consistency of scales, we fix the variance of each observed variable to 1 in our model. This way we standardize the latent variables.

[20] Brown, 2006, p.135.
[21] Brown, 2006, p.134.

In the unstandardized solution, factor loadings can be interpreted as regression coefficients between latent variables and observed variables. An unstandardized factor loading "x" means that one unit change in a latent variable is associated with "x" units change in an observed variable. In case of a standardized solution, factor loadings can be defined as standardized regression coefficients. A standardized factor loading "x" means that one standardized score increase of a latent variable corresponds to "x" standardized scores increase of an observed variable. A squared standardized factor loading provides a variance proportion of an observed variable explained by a corresponding latent variable. Conversely, a variance proportion not explained by a latent factor equals one minus a square of standardized factor loading

$$\varepsilon_i = 1 - \lambda_{ij}^2 \qquad (10)$$

5.6 Model Specification

To perform confirmatory factor analysis, we require prior specification of a factor model. Based on the extensive work done during the qualitative research stage, this model is available.

We have identified earlier that one of the latent factors is "Willingness to integrate into the society with the help of a hearing instrument or an implant". In AMOS, we use the abbreviation HRI (*Hearing Aid Readiness Index*) to indicate this latent variable. The observed variables associated with this factor are the following:

- The need to communicate over the phone ($phone\_use$);
- The need to lead a difficult conversation, such as a conversation with a group of people or a conversation in situations with loud background noise ($dif.Conver$);
- The need to speak often with new people, strangers ($strangers$).

Another factor identified in the qualitative research is "Willingness and ability to borrow". To indicate this latent variable, we use the abbreviation BRI (*Borrowing Readiness Index*). The observed variables for this factor are the following:

- Prior positive experience with aided hearing ($aposterioriqaly\_normal$);
- Willingness and ability to take a formal or an informal loan ($borrow\_normal$);

- Willingness and ability to put up collateral ($sell\_assets$).

The last factor identified in the qualitative research is "Willingness and ability to save". In AMOS, we use the abbreviation SRI (*Saving Readiness Index*) to indicate this latent variable. The observed variables associated with this factor are:

- Sufficient income left after deducting taxes and living expenses ($monthly\_income\_normal$);
- Access to partial or full reimbursement ($reimbursement\_normal$);
- Personal discount rate for the time value of money ($time\_preference\_normal$).

During the qualitative research, we have identified three latent variables, and for each of them – three distinct observed variable. The finding of the qualitative research can be represented by the following system of equations:

$$strangers = \lambda_{11} HRI + \varepsilon_1 \tag{11}$$

$$dif.Conver = \lambda_{21} HRI + \varepsilon_2 \tag{12}$$

$$phone\_use = \lambda_{31} HRI + \varepsilon_3 \tag{13}$$

$$reimbursement\_normal = \lambda_{42} SRI + \varepsilon_4 \tag{14}$$

$$time\_preference\_normal = \lambda_{52} SRI + \varepsilon_5 \tag{15}$$

$$monthly\_income\_normal = \lambda_{62} SRI + \varepsilon_6 \tag{16}$$

$$sell\_assets = \lambda_{73} BRI + \varepsilon_7 \tag{17}$$

$$aposterioriqaly\_normal = \lambda_{83} BRI + \varepsilon_8 \tag{18}$$

$$borrow\_normal = \lambda_{93} BRI + \varepsilon_9 \tag{19}$$

As an input to CFA we use the hypothesized model. The model hypothesized during the qualitative research has only one latent variable per observed variable. Therefore, we observe the same situation in the equations above.

In confirmatory factor analysis, it is possible to define latent variables (factors) either as exogenous or as endogenous. Exogenous variables are not caused by other latent variables in the model. Conversely, endogenous variables are caused by another model factor or by combination of them. Endogenous variables are typically used when a model contains higher order latent variables.

All latent variables in our model are exogenous. Besides, from the qualitative research, we know that each observed variable loads only on one latent variable. Next, we put all factor loadings used in these equations into a matrix Λ:

$$\Lambda = \begin{bmatrix} \lambda_{11} & 0 & 0 \\ \lambda_{21} & 0 & 0 \\ \lambda_{31} & 0 & 0 \\ 0 & \lambda_{42} & 0 \\ 0 & \lambda_{52} & 0 \\ 0 & \lambda_{62} & 0 \\ 0 & 0 & \lambda_{73} \\ 0 & 0 & \lambda_{83} \\ 0 & 0 & \lambda_{93} \end{bmatrix} \tag{20}$$

We assume all measurement errors to be random. This means that the observed relationship between any of two observed variables is entirely caused by a common factor. If we put error residuals of each observed variable in a matrix Θ_ε, we will have the following matrix that depicts measurement errors:

$$\Theta_\varepsilon = \begin{bmatrix} \varepsilon_1 & 0 & 0 & 0 & 0 & 0 & 0 & 0 & 0 \\ 0 & \varepsilon_2 & 0 & 0 & 0 & 0 & 0 & 0 & 0 \\ 0 & 0 & \varepsilon_3 & 0 & 0 & 0 & 0 & 0 & 0 \\ 0 & 0 & 0 & \varepsilon_4 & 0 & 0 & 0 & 0 & 0 \\ 0 & 0 & 0 & 0 & \varepsilon_5 & 0 & 0 & 0 & 0 \\ 0 & 0 & 0 & 0 & 0 & \varepsilon_6 & 0 & 0 & 0 \\ 0 & 0 & 0 & 0 & 0 & 0 & \varepsilon_7 & 0 & 0 \\ 0 & 0 & 0 & 0 & 0 & 0 & 0 & \varepsilon_8 & 0 \\ 0 & 0 & 0 & 0 & 0 & 0 & 0 & 0 & \varepsilon_9 \end{bmatrix} \tag{21}$$

Next, we put factor variances and covariances into a matrix Ψ:

$$\Psi = \begin{bmatrix} 1 & \psi_{2,1} & \psi_{3,1} \\ \psi_{2,1} & 1 & \psi_{3,2} \\ \psi_{3,1} & \psi_{3,2} & 1 \end{bmatrix} \tag{22}$$

Here we exploit the fact that the factor covariance matrix Ψ is symmetric. Besides,

> "In order to conduct CFA, every latent variable must have its scale identified. By nature, latent variables are unobserved and thus have no defined metrics (unit of measurement). Thus, these units of measurement must be set by the researcher."[22]

There are two ways to do this. One is to "fix the metric of the latent variable to be the same as one of its indicators."[23] Another way is "the variance of the latent variable is fixed to a specific value, usually 1.00."[24] In the latter approach, the latent variables are standardized, because their variances are fixed to one. In this research, we chose the latter approach and fixed the variance of each of the three latent variables to one. Therefore, the matrix Ψ has ones on its main diagonal.

Predicted covariances between observed variables can be put in the matrix Σ like this:

$$\Sigma = \begin{bmatrix} \sigma_{11} & \sigma_{12} & \sigma_{13} & \sigma_{14} & \sigma_{15} & \sigma_{16} & \sigma_{17} & \sigma_{18} & \sigma_{19} \\ \sigma_{21} & \sigma_{22} & \sigma_{23} & \sigma_{24} & \sigma_{25} & \sigma_{26} & \sigma_{27} & \sigma_{28} & \sigma_{29} \\ \sigma_{31} & \sigma_{32} & \sigma_{33} & \sigma_{34} & \sigma_{35} & \sigma_{36} & \sigma_{37} & \sigma_{38} & \sigma_{39} \\ \sigma_{41} & \sigma_{42} & \sigma_{43} & \sigma_{44} & \sigma_{45} & \sigma_{46} & \sigma_{47} & \sigma_{48} & \sigma_{49} \\ \sigma_{51} & \sigma_{52} & \sigma_{53} & \sigma_{54} & \sigma_{55} & \sigma_{56} & \sigma_{57} & \sigma_{58} & \sigma_{59} \\ \sigma_{61} & \sigma_{62} & \sigma_{63} & \sigma_{64} & \sigma_{65} & \sigma_{66} & \sigma_{67} & \sigma_{68} & \sigma_{69} \\ \sigma_{71} & \sigma_{72} & \sigma_{73} & \sigma_{74} & \sigma_{75} & \sigma_{76} & \sigma_{77} & \sigma_{78} & \sigma_{79} \\ \sigma_{81} & \sigma_{82} & \sigma_{83} & \sigma_{84} & \sigma_{85} & \sigma_{86} & \sigma_{87} & \sigma_{88} & \sigma_{89} \\ \sigma_{91} & \sigma_{92} & \sigma_{93} & \sigma_{94} & \sigma_{95} & \sigma_{96} & \sigma_{97} & \sigma_{98} & \sigma_{99} \end{bmatrix} \quad (23)$$

CFA iteratively comes up with a predicted covariance matrix Σ. The first step of the first iteration starts with the following equation:

$$S = \Lambda_1 \Psi_1 \Lambda_1' + \Theta_\varepsilon \quad (24)$$

The matrix S is known – it consists of covariances of the observed variables. The matrix Θ_ε is unknown, but it can be easily calculated from the unknown matrix Λ. Error residual, as was mentioned above, equals one minus squared factor loading:

---

[22] Brown, 2006, p. 62.

[23] Brown, 2006, p. 62.

[24] Brown, 2006, p. 63.

$$\varepsilon_i = 1 - \lambda_{ij}^2 \qquad (25)$$

where

- ε_i is the i-th error residual

- λ_{ij} is the loading of the j-th factor on the i-th observed variable.

Harrington (2009) gives the following description of the iterative fitting process in confirmatory factor analysis:

> "The iterative fitting process is similar to having a garment, such as a wedding dress or suit, fitted. You begin with your best guess of what size should fit, and then the tailor assesses the fit and decides if adjustments are needed. If needed, the adjustments are made and then the garment is tried on again. The process continues until some fitting criteria are reached (i.e. the garment fits properly) or some external criteria (i.e. the wedding date) forces the process to stop. If the fitting criteria are reached, then the fit is said to converge and we have a well-fitting garment (or CFA model). But if the fitting criteria are not reached, we may be forced to accept a poorly fitting garment (or CFA model) or to begin again with a new size or style (or a different CFA model). Just as there are multiple tailors available who will use slightly different criteria, there are also multiple estimation methods available for CFA – each with its own advantages and disadvantages."[25]

AMOS 20.0 estimates the unknown matrices Λ_1 and Ψ_1 from the equation (24). The matrices Λ_1 and Ψ_1 are first estimations of the matrices Λ and Ψ respectively.

In the second step of the first iteration, we calculate the first estimate of the matrix Σ, based on the estimates Λ_1 and Ψ_1 obtained in the previous step. Let us call this first estimate Σ_1. We calculate it using the following equation[26]:

$$\Sigma_1 = \Lambda_1 \Psi_1 \Lambda_1' + \Theta_\varepsilon \qquad (26)$$

After Σ_1 is calculated, it is used as a matrix Σ in the formula (7) to calculate the first estimate of F_{WLS}. Let us call it $F_{WLS,1}$.

After the first iteration is complete, the second iteration starts. In the first step of the second iteration, the matrices Λ_2 and Ψ_2 are estimated by taking matrices Λ_1 and Ψ_1 and modifying elements of the matrices a little bit. After that the matrices Λ_2 and Ψ_2 are used to calculate the second estimate of the matrix Σ (let us call it Σ_2):

---

[25] Harrington, 2009, p. 28.

[26] Bollen, 1989.

$$\Sigma_2 = \Lambda_2 \Psi_2 \Lambda_2' + \Theta_\varepsilon \tag{27}$$

After Σ_2 is calculated, it is used as a matrix Σ in the formula (7) to calculate the second estimate of the fitting function F_{WLS}. Let us call it $F_{WLS,2}$. Then the estimate $F_{WLS,2}$ is compared with the estimate $F_{WLS,1}$ to determine which one of the two is smaller. In confirmatory factor analysis, the goal is to minimize the value of the fitting function. Therefore, choosing the smallest value of the fitting function allows selecting the right estimates. Depending on which fitting function value is smaller, the corresponding estimates of the matrices Λ and Ψ are taken as the starting point for the next modification of the estimates of the matrices Λ and Ψ. In all the next steps, the estimates of matrices Λ and Ψ are adjusted, the estimate of the matrix Λ and Ψ and the estimate of the fitting function F_{WLS} are calculated, then compared with the previous estimate and so on.

In our case, AMOS 20.0 notified us that fitting was successful after 10 iterations. In the 10-th iteration, the value of the fitting function was less than 0.00001, which is a default convergence criterion for AMOS 20.0. Therefore, the iterative fitting process stopped and the solution was reported.

Graphically our hypothesized model is depicted on the Figure 27.

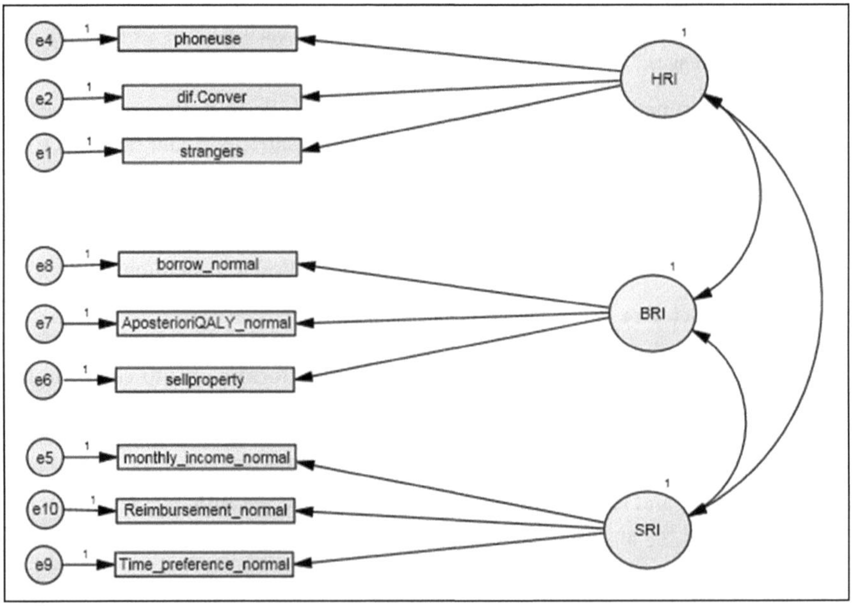

Figure 27: Hypothesized structural equation model.[27]

[27] Own illustration using AMOS 20.0.

To determine if there is a solution to the model, we have to answer the question whether the number of unknowns is bigger or smaller than the number of known pieces of information in the model.

> "A model is under-identified when the number of unknown (freely estimated) parameters exceeds the number of pieces of known information (i.e., elements of the input variance-covariance matrix). An under-identified model cannot be solved because there are an infinite number of parameter estimates that result in perfect model fit. To illustrate, consider the following basic equation:
>
> $$x + y = 7$$
>
> In this instance, there are two unknowns (x and y), and one known ($x + y = 7$). This equation is under-identified because the number of unknown parameters (x and y) exceeds the known information; consequently, there are an infinite number of pairs of values that x and y could take on to solve $x + y = 7$ ($x = 1, y = 6; x = 2, y = 5$ etc.)"[28]

On the other hand,

> "A model is over-identified when the number of knowns (i.e., number of variances and covariances in the input matrix) exceeds the number of freely estimated parameters."[29]

In our research, known variables are variances of the observed variables, and covariances of each pair of the observed variables. As was discussed above, we have 9 observed variables and, therefore, 45 known elements of the variance-covariance matrix S. The unknowns are freely estimated parameters of the model. In our model, we have the following unknown variables: 9 factor loadings $\lambda_{j.m}$, 9 error variances ε_j, and 3 factor covariances. The 3 factor variances were fixed to be $\psi_{i,i} = 1$ and for that reason are not included in the count of unknowns. It leaves us with the total of 21 unknown variables. The difference between the number of known variables and the number of unknown variables gives the model's degrees of freedom (df). In our case, we have 45 known variables and 21 unknown variables. This makes $45 - 21 = 24$ degrees of freedom. Since this number is positive, we can conclude that our model is over-identified with 24 degrees of freedom. However,

> "Over-identified models rarely fit the data perfectly (i.e., a perfectly fitting model is one whose parameter estimates recreate the input variance-covariance matrix exactly)."[30]

---

[28] Brown, 2006, pp. 63-64.
[29] Brown, 2006, p. 67.
[30] Brown, 2006, p. 70.

Therefore,

> "An important aspect of over-identified solutions is that goodness-of-fit evaluation applies – specifically, how well the model is able to reproduce the input variances and covariances (i.e. the input matrix) using a lesser number of unknowns (i.e. freely estimated model parameters)."[31]

5.7 Input Data

The sample consists of 181 entries. All entries were collected by asking the hearing impaired to fill out the online survey. The analyzed data consists of 9 observed variables. The types of the variables are the following:

- Binary variables:
  - *phone_use*;
  - *dif.Conver*;
  - *strangers* ;
  - *sell_assets*;
- Continuous variables:
  - *aposterioriqaly_normal*;
- Categorical variables:
  - *borrow_normal*;
  - *monthly_income_normal*;
  - *reimbursement_normal*;
  - *time_preference_normal*.

All data are complete. As a result, no missing data techniques were employed. The sample variance-covariance matrix S is shown in Table 4.

[31] Brown, 2006, p. 70.

Table 4: Sample variance-covariance matrix.

	Reimbursement_normal	Time_preference_normal	borrow_normal	AposterioriQALY_normal	sellproperty	monthly_income_normal	phoneuse	dif.Conver	strangers
Reimburse-ment_normal	0,176								
Time_ preference_ normal	0,023	0,136							
borrow_ normal	0,023	0,007	0,138						
Aposteriori QALY_ normal	0,01	0,015	0,036	0,051					
sellproperty	–0,009	–0,01	0,041	0,023	0,207				
monthly_ income_ normal	0,029	0,01	0,03	0,008	0,017	0,057			
phoneuse	–0,008	0,01	0,019	0,017	0,015	0,005	0,146		
dif.Conver	0,022	0,021	0,046	0,027	0,005	0,026	0,061	0,246	
Strangers	0,005	0,007	0,015	0,011	0,018	0,015	0,054	0,089	0,229

Here, on the main diagonal the variances of the observed variables are shown. The numbers outside the main diagonal are covariances of the corresponding observed variables.

The covariance q_{xy} between any of two variables x and y is calculated using the following formula:

$$q_{xy} = \frac{1}{n-1} \sum (x_i - \bar{x})(y_i - \bar{y}) \tag{28}$$

where

- x_i and y_i equate to i-th observations of the corresponding variables;
- n is the number of observations of the variables x and y;
- $\bar{x}$ is the mean of the variable x;
- $\bar{y}$ is the mean of the variable y.

Table 5: Sample correlation matrix.

	Reimbursement_normal	Time_preference_normal	borrow_normal	AposterioriQALY_normal	sellproperty	monthly_income_normal	phoneuse	dif.Conver	strangers
Reimburse-ment_normal	1								
Time_ preference_ normal	0,152	1							
borrow_normal	0,145	0,052	1						
Aposteriori QALY_normal	0,107	0,186	0,427	1					
sellproperty	–0,049	–0,062	0,241	0,227	1				
monthly_ income_normal	0,289	0,119	0,334	0,151	0,159	1			
phoneuse	–0,052	0,071	0,132	0,199	0,084	0,057	1		
dif.Conver	0,106	0,112	0,249	0,239	0,021	0,218	0,322	1	
strangers	0,025	0,041	0,082	0,102	0,083	0,135	0,293	0,374	1

The sample correlation matrix is shown in Table 5. Here, in each cell the correlation between variables is shown. The correlation r_{xy} between any of two variables x and y is calculated using the following formula:

$$r_{xy} = \frac{n\sum x_i y_i - \sum x_i \sum y_i}{\sqrt{n\sum x_i^2 - (\sum x_i)^2}\sqrt{n\sum y_i^2 - (\sum y_i)^2}} \qquad (29)$$

where

- x_i and y_i equate to i-th observations of the corresponding variables;
- n is the number of observations of the variables x and y.

The assessment of normality of the observed variables is presented in Table 6. As shown in this table, for every observed variable we have minimum and maximum value, skewness, skewness critical ratio, kurtosis, and kurtosis critical ratio.

Table 6: The assessment of normality of the observed variables.

Variable	min	max	skew	c.r.	kurtosis	c.r.
Reimbursement_normal	0	1	0,771	4,233	–1,199	–3,294
Time_preference_normal	0	1	–0,792	–4,352	–0,799	–2,193
borrow_normal	0	1	1,088	5,978	–0,418	–1,147
AposterioriQALY_normal	0	1	–0,353	–1,938	–0,233	–0,64
Sellproperty	0	1	0,911	5,001	–1,171	–3,215
monthly_income_normal	0	1	1,316	7,226	1,023	2,809
Phone_use	0	1	1,694	9,306	0,871	2,392
dif.Conver	0	1	0,256	1,407	–1,934	–5,312
Strangers	0	1	0,612	3,364	–1,625	–4,462

Skewness is a measure of asymmetry, or more precisely, the lack of symmetry of the probability distribution of a variable. A negative skewness value indicates that the majority of values of a variable lie to the right of the mean. A positive skewness value suggests that the majority of values of a variable lie to the left of the mean. A zero value indicates a symmetric distribution. For a sample of *n* observations of a variable *x*, the skewness is calculated using the formula:

$$skew_x = \frac{\frac{1}{n}\sum(x_i - \bar{x})^3}{(\frac{1}{n}\sum(x_i - \bar{x})^2)^{\frac{3}{2}}} \qquad (30)$$

where

- n is the number of observations of the variable x;
- x_i is the i-th observation of the variable x;
- $\bar{x}$ is the mean of the variable x.

Kurtosis is a measure of "peakedness" of the probability distribution of a variable. The higher the kurtosis is the more of the variance is the result of rare extreme deviations. This also means that the peak of a distribution is sharp and, at the same time, the tail is fat. Such distribution is called leptokurtic. Low kurtosis implies that deviations are frequent and modestly sized. In this case, the peak is rounded, and the tail is short. This distribution is called platykurtic. For a sample of *n* observations of a variable *x*, kurtosis is calculated using the formula:

$$kurtosis_x = \frac{\frac{1}{n}\sum(x_i - \bar{x})^4}{(\frac{1}{n}\sum(x_i - \bar{x})^2)^2} - 3 \quad (31)$$

where

- n is the number of observations of the variable x;
- x_i is the i-th observation of the variable x;
- $\bar{x}$ is the mean of the variable x.

West et al. (1995) proposed as a measure for testing for substantial departure of normality the following indicators:

- Absolute skewness value higher than 2, or
- Absolute kurtosis value higher than 7, or
- For a sample size ($50 < n < 300$) the absolute value of z-score of skewness and kurtosis values has to be larger than 3.29.

If any of these criteria are satisfied, we can state that the distribution of a given variable is not normal. In our case, AMOS 20.0 reports an excess kurtosis instead of a proper kurtosis by automatically subtracting three from each absolute kurtosis value (Table 6). Both skewness and excess kurtosis have to be equal to zero for a perfect normal distribution. Therefore, we have to check for the absolute kurtosis value larger than four[32] to satisfy the criteria of the substantial departure of normality. The Table 6 also contains the critical ratios for both skewness and kurtosis. These ratios are calculated by dividing skewness and kurtosis by their standard deviations respectively. Both critical ratios are interpreted as z-scores. In our case, the sample size n=181, thus, the criteria of absolute value of z-score being larger than 3.29 is applicable.

To verify if the substantial departure of normality criteria is satisfied, we look at the the Table 6 and check skewness, kurtosis, and critical ratios for each of the observed variables. All variables except *aposterioriqaly_normal* have the absolute values of at least one of their critical ratios larger than 3.29. Therefore, we can conclude that the observed variables *phone_use*, *dif.conver*, *strangers*, *borrow_normal*, *sell_assets*, *monthly_income_normal*, *reimbursement _normal*, *time_preference_normal* are not normally distributed.

[32] Absolute kurtosis value threshold of 7 minus 3 to get the excess kurtosis equals to 4 as the upper threshold for excess kurtosis.

5.8 Model Evaluation

CFA provides information on how well the hypothesized model fits the real world data. For evaluation of adequacy of model fit, the following statistics are used:

- χ^2;
- Steiger's root mean square error of approximation (RMSEA);
- Comparative fit index (CFI);
- Tucker-Lewis index (TLI);
- Root mean square residual (RMR);
- Goodness-of-fit (GIF);
- Adjusted goodness-of-fit (AGIF);
- Parsimony goodness-of-fit (PGIF).

χ^2 is a classic goodness-of-fit index. It is calculated using the following formula:

$$\chi^2 = \sum_{i=1}^{n}\sum_{j=1}^{n}\frac{(s_{ij} - \sigma_{ij})^2}{s_{ij}} \tag{32}$$

where

- s_{ij} is an element of a matrix S located on an i-th row and a j-th column;
- σ_{ij} is an element of a matrix Σ located on an i-th row and a j-th column;
- n is a number of observed variables.

χ^2 reflects the statistical goodness-of-fit of the observed data compared to the hypothesized model. Jöreskog (1970) suggested adjusting values of χ^2 by the degrees of freedom. He argued that it simplifies assessing model fit for various models. The adjusted value of χ^2 should not exceed 5.0 for a model to truly represent the observed data.[33] Carmines and McIver (1981) suggested the upper threshold to be either 2.0 or 3.0.

In our case, indices i and j iterate both from one to nine as $n = 9$. It means that $\chi^2 = 31.195$. To receive a more meaningful adjusted value of χ^2, we divide it by the degrees of freedom. As mentioned above, our model has 24 degrees of

33 Jöreskog, 1970.

freedom. Therefore, the adjusted value in our situation is 1.3. This is good, because it is below the upper threshold of 2.0.

To assess the goodness-of-fit of our model, we also use the p-value. It shows the probability that the deviations of the observed data from the hypothesized model are due to chance alone, not other factors. The higher the p-value the better our model fits the reality. In our case, p-value is 0.148. It is above the significance level of 0.05. Therefore, we have a good model fit.

χ^2 is rarely used in applied research as a sole index of model fit because of its high sensitivity to a sample size. Besides, it is based on a very stringent hypothesis that $\Sigma = S$.[34] While $\chi^2$is routinely reported in CFA research, other fit indices are relied on more for purposes of evaluation of model fit.

Another commonly used statistics is the Root Mean Square Error of Approximation (RMSEA). It relies on noncentral χ^2distribution. This type of distribution of the fitting function can be observed when the model fit is not perfect. The RMSEA assesses the extent to which a model fits reasonably well in a population. Since it is a population-based index, it is relatively insensitive to sample size. Its upper range is unbounded, but it rarely exceeds 1.0. A RMSEA value of 0.0 indicates a perfect fit. A value less than 0.5 suggests a good model fit. Besides RMSEA value, the probability value (p-value) should be checked to confirm non-significance ($p>0.05$). Jöreskog and Sörbom (1996) propose a stricter guideline: $p>0.5$. In our case, the RMSEA index equals 0.041, and its probability is 0.619. These all imply a good model fit.

Comparative fit index (CFI) evaluates fit of a hypothesized model in relation to a more restricted, nested baseline model. Typically, a baseline model has correlations among all input variables fixed to zero. Byrne (1994) proposes to use CFI as a primary index when evaluating a model fit. CFI has a range of possible values from 0.0 to 1.0. The values closer to 1.0 imply a good model fit. We have comparative fit index equal 0.937. Therefore, our model fits the obsereved data well.

Tucker-Lewis index (TLI) is another comparative fit index widely used in confirmatory factor analysis literature. It can be interpreted in a fashion similar to the comparative fit index. Values above 0.9 mean good model fit. As TLI is non-normed, it can also have values outside the range of 0.0 to 1.0. In our case, TLI=0.905, which confirmes good model fit.

The root mean square residual (RMR) represents the average residual value derived from fitting the hypothesized model to the sample data. The standardized RMR ranges between 0.0 and 1.0. The value less than 0.05 indicates a good model fit. In our case RMR=0.009. It implies one more time that our model has a

34 Brown, 2006.

good fit. It also indicates that the model explains the sample data correlations with an average error of 0.009.

Next useful indices are GFI (goodness-of-fit) and AGFI (adjusted goodness-of-fit). They are absolute indices of fit, because they compare the hypothesized model with the no model at all.[35] Both indices range from 0.0 to 1.0. The values higher than 0.9 imply a good fit model. The value of 1.0 indicates a perfect fit. In our case, GFI=0.993, while AGFI=0.987. We have confirmed once again the good fit of our model.

PGFI (parsimony goodness-of-fit index) takes into account the number of estimated parameters of the hypothesized model during the assessment of the overall fit. Therefore, PGFI provides via one index both the information on the goodness of fit and the parsimony of the model. Mulaik et al. (1989) suggests that the values of PGFI above 0.5 shall be considered acceptable, provided other indicators suggest a good or a perfect model fit. In our case, PGFI=0.530, other indicators suggest at least good model fit, thus PGFI value is also acceptable.

Although goodness-of-fit statistics provide sufficient information on the global fit of the model, it is possible that there are some localized areas of ill fit. If such areas exist, they need to be highlighted. Under localized areas of ill fit we understand that a relationship among certain observed variables is not reproduced adequately in the hypthesized model. There are two CFA statistics, which are used to show areas of misfit. They are residuals and modification indices.

First, we take a look at the residual variance-covariance matrix. This matrix shows the difference between the sample variance-covariance matrix (S) and variance-covariance matrix (Σ) predicted by the model. Analyzing the residual matrix, we can see how well each of the observed variables' variance and covariance was reproduced by the hypothesized model. To account for different measurement scales of variables, AMOS 20.0 provides only the standardized residual variance-covariance matrix. It is calculated by dividing each unstandartized residual by its estimated standard error. The standardized residual variance-covariance matrix is shown in the Table 7. In the table, a positive standardized residual means that the model parameters underestimate the relationship between the observed variables. If a standardized residual value is large and positive, additional parameters should be added to a model to better account for covariance between observed variables. Conversely, a negative standardized residual means that model parameters overestimate the relationship between observed variables. Large negative standardized residuals signal that a model overestimates the observed relationship between a pair of variables. Due to the fact that standized residuals can be roughly interpreted as a Z-score, with a correct model

[35] Hu & Bentler, 1995.

Table 7: The standardized residual variance-covariance matrix.

	Reimbursement_normal	Time_preference_normal	borrow_normal	AposterioriQALY_normal	sellproperty	monthly_income_normal	phoneuse	dif.Conver	strangers
Reimburse-ment_ normal	0,822								
Time_ preference_ normal	0,944	-0,005							
borrow_ normal	0,467	-0,323	0,166						
Aposteriori QALY_ normal	0,046	1,639	-0,42	1,168					
sellproperty	-1,525	-1,381	-0,26	-0,231	0,176				
monthly_ income_ normal	-0,204	-1,166	0,791	-1,447	0,187	0,31			
phoneuse	-1,629	0,476	-0,39	0,762	-0,01	-1,178	1,465		
dif.Conver	0,44	0,83	0,486	0,579	-1,24	0,449	-0,18	0,199	
strangers	-0,536	-0,027	-1,3	-0,903	-0,16	-0,275	0,177	0,006	0,293

most standardized residuals should be less than 1.96 in absolute value in order to be acceptable.[36] The value of 1.96 is chosen, because it corresponds to a statistically significant Z-score at $p<0.05$. The Table 7 shows that this criterion is satisfied for our model. Therefore we can conclude the absence of localized areas of misfit in the solution. The relationships between the observed variables are not statistically significantly underestimated or overestimated.

Continuing with localized areas of ill fit analysis, we take a look at modification indices. The modification index shows how much the overall χ^2 of a model would decrease if a specific parameter was freely estimated instead of fixed or constrained. A good fitting model shall produce small modification indices. On

36 Jöreskog & Sörbom, 1996.

Table 8: Modification indices for covariances of error residuals.

			M.I.	**Par Change**
e9	<-->	e10	0,376	0,005
e7	<-->	e8	0,02	0
e6	<-->	e8	0,235	-0,004
e6	<-->	e7	0,578	0,004
e5	<-->	e10	0,032	0,001
e5	<-->	e9	0,208	-0,002
e2	<-->	e4	0,72	-0,007
e1	<-->	e4	1,308	0,01
e1	<-->	e2	0	0

the conceptual level, modification indices can be imagined as χ^2 statistics with one degree of freedom. The modification index that corresponds to the critical value of χ^2 at $p < 0.5$ and one degree of freedom shall be higher than 3.84. If such modification indices are present, an overall model fit can be statistically significantly improved by freely estimating fixed parameters that correspond to these modification indices.

Having said all this, there are not so many parameters where we can add regression lines. The regression lines between observed and latent variables are already defined in our model. Therefore, we do not examine the regression weights modification indices, but only look at the modification indices for covariances. It would not make sense to try to covary error residuals with observed or latent variables, as this would defy the logic behind the error residuals. They are residuals, while they are not explained by other observed or latent variables. Likewise, it does not make sense to covary error residuals of variables loaded on different latent variables. We can only covary error residuals of observed variables loaded on the same factor. Modification indices for covariances of error residuals are shown in the Table 8.

In Table 8, modification indices and a parameter change for each given pair of error residuals. The value of modification index (M.I.) shows that if we repeat the analysis treating a covariance between unique errors of 2 variables as a free parameter, instead of a fixed parameter, discrepancy will decrease. The reduction will be equal to a value of a corresponding modification index. Discrepancy is χ^2 statistics, which show the difference between sample data and an estimated model. A parameter change value indicates how much a covariance between two error residuals will change if it is freely estimated. As seen from Table 8, no pair of error residuals shows a statistically significant increase in the model fit if a covariance between them is freely estimated instead of being fixed.

Having analysed localized areas of ill fit, the next step is to check if all parameters of the model are really necessary. If the model contains any statistically

Table 9: Regression weights.

			Estimate	S.E.	C.R.	P
strangers	<---	HRI	0,268	0,039	6,78	***
dif.Conver	<---	HRI	0,331	0,032	10,236	***
phoneuse	<---	HRI	0,191	0,038	5,029	***
sellproperty	<---	BRI	0,169	0,036	4,728	***
AposterioriQALY_normal	<---	BRI	0,148	0,017	8,845	***
borrow_normal	<---	BRI	0,261	0,028	9,419	***
Time_preference_normal	<---	SRI	0,088	0,03	2,967	0,003
Reimbursement_normal	<---	SRI	0,147	0,037	4,002	***
monthly_income_normal	<---	SRI	0,206	0,044	4,715	***

insignificant parameters, then this would be a sign that it could be further improved by fixing statistically insignificant factor loadings to 0. Statistical significance of any of freely estimated parameters can be calculated by dividing the unstandardized parameter estimate by its standard error. This ratio is called critical ratio (C.R.) and can be interpreted as a z-score. The absolute value over 1.96 indicates statistical significance of a freely estimated parameter. 1.96 is a value that corresponds to 95% probability of parameter insignificance. Thus, if a critical ratio value is below 1.96, the parameter is statistically insignificant and can be removed from the model. In Table 9, estimates of regression weights, their standard errors, C.R. and probabilities are shown. Probability column value of "***" indicates that the probability value is less than 0.001.

A value of probability less than 0.05 means that a parameter is significant. By examining critical ratio and probability columns in Table 9, we see that all regression weights between observed and latent variables are significant. Therefore, all observed variables in our model are statistically significantly related to their corresponding latent variables.

Now, we can proceed to inspecting the direction, magnitude and significance of the parameter estimates. Let us take a closer look at factor loadings, factor covariances and error residuals of the observed variables. Here, we look for out-of-range values. Dillon et al. (1987) call situations with out-of-range values Heywood cases. If Heywood cases occur, the CFA model shall not be deemed acceptable.[37] Heywood cases are impossible to obtain if you are calculating such values like variance or standardized value directly from the corresponding formula. But in CFA, where such values like error variances or factor loadings are iteratively estimated, it is possible to obtain such out-of-range values. There are different reasons why Heywood cases occur. For example, outliers in

[37] Brown, 2006.

Table 10: Error variances.

	Estimate	S.E.	C.R.	P
e1	0,15	0,022	6,757	***
e2	0,131	0,023	5,778	***
e4	0,089	0,016	5,723	***
e5	0,012	0,016	0,766	0,444
e6	0,175	0,016	10,938	***
e7	0,024	0,005	4,862	***
e8	0,067	0,013	5,231	***
e9	0,128	0,01	13,423	***
e10	0,14	0,015	9,634	***

the input data and structurally misspecified models are possible causes for Heywood cases.[38] Empirical underidentification is another possible cause.[39]

Heywood cases manifest themselves in the following ways:

- Negative factor variances
- Negative error variances
- Standardized factor loadings with a value greater than 1 in cases where each observed variable loads on exactly one latent variable

In our case, factor variances were all fixed to one from the very beginning, so it is by definition not relevant to our model. Error variances of our model are shown in Table 10 in the column "Estimate". As can be seen in the table, all error variances in our model are non-negative. In addition, we can also analyze standard errors of error variances (in the column "S.E."), critical ratio (in the column "C.R."; critical ratio is calculated as error variance divided by standard error) and probabilities. A probability value of "***" means that it is less than 0.001. Examining critical ratios of error variances, we see that all of them, except ε_5, are statistically significant. An error variance is considered statistically significant if its critical ratio is larger than 1.96, which corresponds to 95% confidence interval. Nevertheless, nonsignificant error variances should not instigate remedial activity and, in fact, signify that an observed variable is very strongly related to its latent factor.[40]

Last, we examine standardized regression weights on values greater than 1. In Table 11 standardized regression weights of observed variables on latent vari-

[38] Bollen, 1987.

[39] Rindskopf, 1984.

[40] Brown, 2006.

Table 11: Standardized regression weights.

			Estimate
strangers	<---	HRI	0,568
dif.Conver	<---	HRI	0,675
phoneuse	<---	HRI	0,539
sellproperty	<---	BRI	0,375
AposterioriQALY_normal	<---	BRI	0,693
borrow_normal	<---	BRI	0,709
Time_preference_normal	<---	SRI	0,239
Reimbursement_normal	<---	SRI	0,366
monthly_income_normal	<---	SRI	0,88

ables are shown. There are no regression weight values greater than 1. Thus, we can conclude that our model does not contain Heywood cases.

With this, the evaluation of model fit is finished. Based on all said above, we can conclude that our model fits the data well. On the Table 12 95% confidence intervals of factor loadings are shown.

Table 12: 95% confidence intervals of factor loadings.

			95% confidence interval lower boundary	95% confidence interval upper boundary
strangers	<---	HRI	0,19156	0,34444
dif.Conver	<---	HRI	0,26828	0,39372
phoneuse	<---	HRI	0,11652	0,26548
sellproperty	<---	BRI	0,09844	0,23956
AposterioriQALY_normal	<---	BRI	0,11468	0,18132
borrow_normal	<---	BRI	0,20612	0,31588
Time_preference_normal	<---	SRI	0,0292	0,1468
Reimbursement_normal	<---	SRI	0,07448	0,21952
monthly_income_normal	<---	SRI	0,11976	0,29224

6 Substantive Conclusions and Final Recommendations

After having analized the CFA output, we have reached the conclusion that the originally hypothesized model of financing social inclusion of the hearing impaired is confirmed quantitatively. The first finding is that not all hearing impaired will equally benefit from aided hearing. The hearing impaired who often need to use their hearing ability while speaking over the phone, holding a conversation in areas with a lot of background noise, participating in group discussions or talking often with strangers will gain the most. Least of all will benefit the hearing impaired who are fully integrated in deaf society, and those who communicate with normal-hearing people only occasionally in one-on-one conversations. The hearing impaired with high income, who have high subjective time-value-of-money discount rate and access to at least partial reimbursement, are in a better position to afford aided hearing though savings. On the other hand, the hearing impaired who are satisfied with their prior aided hearing experience, are willing to borrow money and put up some of their assets as collateral, are best positioned to afford aided hearing through borrowing.

Practically, our research suggests two viable additions or alternatives to "standard" partial lump-sum reimbursement of hearing instruments or implants. One is creating a special savings account to finance a part or the whole purchase of hearing aids. Another one is a subsidized loan to cover at least a part of expenses associated with aided hearing.

The majority of the hearing impaired in the world do not have access to reimbursements which allow them to buy hearing instruments or implants. Many countries, among them Ukraine and Russia, do not offer a free-of-charge hearing instrument or an implant to every hearing impaired person. Since some of the hearing impaired in Ukraine and Russia receive free-of-charge hearing aids, we can conclude that the rationing of financial help for the hearing impaired is taking place. Healthcare rationing is not a new concept. If all patients sought a medical advice before purchasing non-prescription drugs, the United States of America would need 25 times the number of primary care physicians it currently has.[1] If a visit to a physician were free of charge, we would definitely see the number of visits rise. Similarly, if hearing instruments and implants were free of charge, we would witness much higher hearing aid adoption rates. The UK, due to free-of-charge offering of hearing instruments to all hearing impaired via National

---

1 Rottenberg, 1990.

Health Service, has 38.6% of the hearing impaired who use hearing aids.[2] At the same time, the USA, having only health savings account but no reimbursement for the hearing impaired, has 24.6% of the hearing impaired who use hearing aids. What we do not know is if and how many people who have hearing aids actually use them in their daily life. If hearing instruments were offered free-of-charge, all rational hearing impaired would attempt to get hearing aids as long as the expected benefit is higher than the opportunity cost of time spent on getting it.

Each hearing loss and life circumstances are unique. Some hearing impaired will be satisfied even with the cheapest trimmer device. For others a more expensive computer programmed hearing instrument is better. There are those who want a hearing instrument with Bluetooth connection to stream TV sound signals directly into hearing devices. Yet, some do not need a hearing instrument at all, because they are accustomed to communicating with sign language. Therefore, offering fixed reimbursement is not efficient. In fact, it is a classical moral hazard situation. It can often lead to over-reimbursing or under-reimbursing the needs of a hearing impaired person. In many cases, only the hearing impaired are in a position to make the right choice, perhaps not directly, but rather under professional guidance.

The United States introduced Medical Savings Accounts (MSA) in 1996. These accounts targeted self-employed and employees of small companies (less than 50 employees). MSAs did not get much traction in the US mostly because of consumers' unfamiliarity with the new type of healthcare policy.[3] In 2003 Health Savings Accounts (HSA) were introduced as a replacement and extension of MSA. HSAs were made available also to employees of larger employers. They make account owners responsible for spending decisions on healthcare below high-expense "catastrophic" cases. When costs are shared with patients, the moral hazard problem significantly diminishes.[4]

> "With HSAs, people will not spend a dollar on health care services unless they get a dollar's worth of value. In this respect, HSAs greatly improve patients' incentives."[5]

On a related note Goodman (2006) indicates that experience with HRA (Health Reimbursement Accounts) in the United States and MSA (Medical Savings Account) in South Africa suggests that

> "Patients cut back in areas where there is presumed to be a lot of waste and substitute less expensive treatment options for more expensive ones. That is, there are fewer trips

2 Hougaard & Ruf, 2010.
3 Lyke & Peterson, 2003.
4 Manning et al., 1987.
5 Goodman, 2006, p. 3.

> to primary care physicians; brand-name drug purchases are down; generic purchases are up, etc."[6]

For the hearing impaired this means buying products of low-end brands and private labels instead of premium brands, finding a cost-effective hearing care professional, and choosing between monaural and binaural fitting.

The United States, Singapore, China, and South Africa are the countries with experience in Health Savings Accounts.[7] In addition to HSA described above, there are other types of special savings accounts for financing healthcare in the United States healthcare system. There are various types of them including, but not limited to, Health Reimbursement Accounts (HRA), Medical Savings Account (MSA), Medical Flexible Spending Account (medical FSA) etc. Although different in their setup and terms, all of these dedicated healthcare savings accounts share the same two characteristics relevant to our research. First, they are designed to give account owners strong incentives to use accumulated funds only on healthcare expenditures. Second, they are designed to ensure that account owners would prefer financing their healthcare expenses through these accounts and not other ones.

A HSA is a tax-advantaged savings plan with minimum deductibles of 1200 USD for single coverage and 2400 USD for family coverage in 2011.[8] Consumers, family members, and employers can make deposits into a tax-favored account (up to annual limits) for qualified medical expenses. Funds deposited to a HSA are not subject to taxation at the time of deposit. Money withdrawal from a HSA is not subject to taxation if used on qualified medical expenses. The withdrawal does not necessarily have to be within any defined period of time. Besides, one may invest HSA funds. Earnings on such investments are protected from taxation until money withdrawal. If money is withdrawn on qualified health expenses, then the withdrawal will remain tax-free.

All other healthcare savings accounts are quite similar to HSAs. A Health Reimbursement Account (HRA) is different from an HSA only by the fact that only an employer is allowed to fund an HRA, while an HSA can be funded not only by employers but also by consumers and family members. Medical Flexible Spending Accounts differ from HSAs in that all funds deposited to them during the year have to be consumed, or otherwise they are lost. On the other hand, money on an HSA can be rolled over an indefinite number of times.

Although an HSA is more cost-effective then full reimbursement, it remains unclear whether introduction of an HSA instead of normal reimbursement increases or decreases the total healthcare expenditure. The extensive study by

6 Goodman, 2006, p. 3.

7 Schreyögg, 2003.

8 AHIP Center for Policy and Research, 2008.

Ozanna (1996) shows that HSAs lead to 2-8% decrease in healthcare spending. It is achieved by giving individuals incentives to look for more cost-effective healthcare. Matisson (2002) also finds that people with HSAs aim for the most cost-effective solutions to their health problems.

The higher the individual's income level the more attractive the participation in an HSA will be for her/him.[9] This is due to the fact that with income growth, tax savings generated by a HSA also grow. Nevertheless, even in the absence of tax incentives, people with higher income tend to save more. We confirm this insight also in our research, because the factor "Willingness and ability to save" is significantly correlated with the observed variable, which describes income level of the hearing impaired.

The hearing impaired who have access to full reimbursement or those who have enough money to afford aided hearing do not necessarily need a subsidized saving solution. A savings account to finance at least part of aided hearing expenses, similar to an HSA, is an attractive option for those hearing impaired who cannot afford aided hearing right now, but who have high enough income to be able to save, low subjective time-value-of-money discount rate and access to partial reimbursement. Such hearing impaired will value incentives of a tax-advantaged money deposit, investment and withdrawal for qualified expenses on aided hearing. Intuitively we can see the reason behind that. When the hearing impaired have relatively high income and low subjective time-value-of-money, they tend to have funds available to save. A savings account for aided hearing will serve as a vehicle to channel these savings towards affordable aided hearing.

Currently, healthcare systems around the world do not offer subsidized loans for financing at least part of the costs associated with aided hearing. The nearest equivalent of such program exists in the United States in form of college loans. Typically, in such loans no interest is accrued while a student remains enrolled in education. After a sixth month grace period, repayment and interest accrual starts. A similar subsidized loan for financing at least part of the costs associated with aided hearing could be very helpful to the hearing impaired who are satisfied with their prior aided hearing experience, willing to borrow money and put up some of their assets as collateral.

The question remains open, how to combine subsidized savings accounts and subsidized loans in practice. In order to answer this question, a microeconomic model of such a combination is described.

We model a cohort of hearing impaired people with the same given degree of hearing loss. These people, due to the nature of their hearing loss, need the same hearing aid (hearing instrument or hearing implant) solution to hear better. Besides, we assume that each person needs only one hearing aid. Let us further

9 Glied & Remler, 2005.

assume that the market price for this hearing aid is the same for all hearing impaired, and is equal to C. We surmise that all hearing impaired in our cohort are willing to obtain aided hearing. The assumption is that everyone of them has her/his own monetary value assigned to the hearing aid, and is willing and able to pay it. This value depends not only on the income and wealth of the hearing impaired person, but also on her/his perception of the handicap caused by unaided hearing loss. Besides, it also depends on the presence of other items such as food, clothing, housing costs etc. that compete with the hearing aid for the share of the hearing impaired person's wallet.

In the absence of any external help, the market demand for hearing solutions is downward sloping. It is depicted in Figure 28 with the curve D. The demand for aided hearing can be represented by the following equation:

$$P = a - bQ \tag{33}$$

where

- a is the price of hearing aids when demanded quantity is 0;
- P is the price a hearing impaired person is willing and able to pay for the hearing aid;
- Q is the quantity of the hearing aids demanded;
- b is the slope of the demand curve.

This equation shows that at different prices different number of the hearing impaired are able to afford aided hearing. We assume that the hearing aid suppliers can provide all hearing impaired in our cohort with it at a given market price C. This assumption is quite realistic, because our group of the hearing impaired is a very small subset of the worldwide population of all hearing impaired. On the other hand, hearing aids manufacturing industry operates on the worldwide economies of scale. Thus, even big changes in demand by our cohort do not make any significant impact on the global hearing aids demand, and therefore cannot influence the prices. Consequently, even though the global supply curve for hearing aids is upward sloping, for our group of the hearing impaired it is flat. Thus, we have a perfectly elastic supply curve S. In case when external help is not available, the equilibrium will be achieved at the point, where Q_N hearing impaired will get aided hearing. Each of them will pay the market price C. Figure 28 depicts the microeconomic situation of the hearing impaired without any external financial help. The vertical axis shows the amount of money in US dollars, and the horizontal axis shows the number of the hearing impaired.

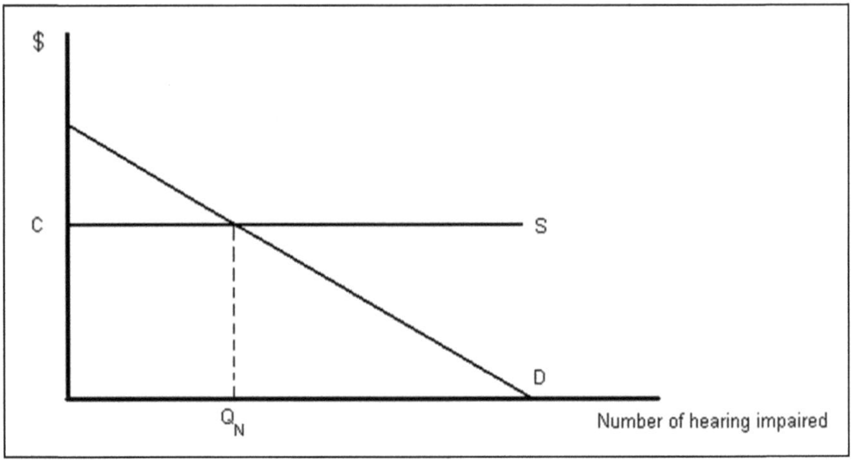

Figure 28: Supply and demand for hearing aids.[10]

Traditional reimbursement aims at increasing the amount of the hearing impaired who can afford aided hearing. We assume that every hearing impaired can get a partial lump-sum reimbursement of aided hearing costs. In money terms, this lump-sum equals *R*. It is given only to those hearing impaired who have enough money to buy hearing aids with its help. If a hearing impaired person cannot afford or is not willing to buy a hearing aid even combined with the partial lump-sum reimbursement, he/she does not get the money. The presence of such reimbursement policy increases the amount of aided hearing impaired from Q_N to Q_R. This is achieved by shifting the demand curve *D* to the right. The new demand curve is called D_R. The equation of this demand curve is

$$P = a + R - bQ \tag{34}$$

where

- *R* is the partial lump-sum reimbursement.

Figure 29 depicts the microeconomic situation of the hearing impaired with a partial lump-sum reimbursement.

[10] Own illustration using MS Paint 5.1.

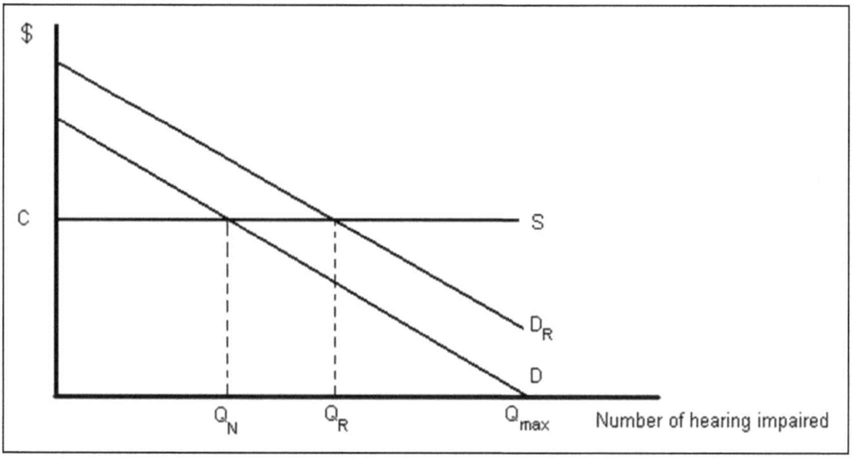

Figure 29: Supply and demand for hearing aids taking into account partial lump-sum reimbursement.[11]

It shows that the lump-sum reimbursement policy costs the payer RQ_R and allows to increase the number of aided hearing impaired by $Q_R - Q_N$ people. Let us assume that the total population of the cohort of the hearing impaired willing to buy aided hearing is Q_{max}.The part of the total cohort population $Q_{\max} - Q_R$ is still not able to afford aided hearing. In Figure 29 Q_{max} is the intersection point of the demand curve D with the abscissa. In other words, if hearing aids were free of charge, Q_{max} people would get aided hearing.

Next, we look at the situation with loans. In our case, the loan subsidy can practically come in a form of loan guarantees and/or a subsidized interest rate. We assume that the budget to support aided hearing is constant. Therefore, the total budget of RQ_R is used now on subsidized loans. The subsidized loans for the hearing aid purchase are given only to those who can afford to pay back. This means that now the hearing impaired have two options: to buy the hearing aid using their own money or to buy it with the help of the subsidized loan. Karlan and Zinman (2005) show that "price elasticity of demand for consumer credit is downward sloping but relatively flat."[12] Therefore, the demand for the second option is more elastic than the demand for the hearing aid alone. In case with the subsidized loans, the demand for aided hearing changes from the demand curve D to another demand function. Let us call this demand curve D_L. We know several things about the new demand function D_L.

[11] Own illustration using MS Paint 5.1.

[12] Karlan & Zinman, 2005, p. 18.

First, it has a flatter slope than the original demand function D. The slope of the new demand function is b_L. Here $b_L < b$, because with the introduction of subsidized loans, the demand for aided hearing becomes more elastic.

Second, the subsidy covers partially the total costs of the loan. Under the total cost of the loan we understand the sum of all payments that need to be done by a borrower to repay the loan on top of the repayment of the borrowed money. This includes interest payments, fees, penalties, and all other payments, but does not include the repayment of the originally borrowed sum of money. Still, the subsidy does not cover all the fees, penalties and interest payments. There are some costs of the loan that are born by the hearing impaired. This condition is necessary to ensure that the hearing impaired, who are able to afford aided hearing, do not take the loan in order to reduce the price of their hearing aid. Therefore, a rational hearing impaired person (those Q_O of the hearing impaired in our cohort with the highest willingness to pay), who is able to pay the price of the hearing aid out of her/his own pocket, will not apply for the subsidized loan to buy the hearing aid, as it will effectively increase the price paid for aided hearing.

Let us call the monetary value of the loan subsidy R_L. Let us further assume that it is smaller than the partial lump-sum reimbursement. Thus, $R_L < R$. This is a valid assumption, because my research shows that in Ukraine and Russia many people with stable income are eligible for a standard consumer loan even without subsidies. Adding subsidies will give additional incentives for people to take loans, and decrease the likelihood of a default on the consumer loan.

Let us further assume that the Q_N people with the highest willingness to pay, who are able to purchase hearing aids with their own funds consist of two subgroups: those, who are able to pay for hearing aids completely out of the pocket, and those, who use a standard (unsubsidized) consumer loan in order to afford aided hearing. The assumption is that the first subgroup has a higher ability to pay than those, who are able to purchase the hearing aid only with a standard consumer loan. This assumption is valid, because the hearing impaired, who do not need the loan, can increase their ability to pay even higher by applying for the standard consumer loan.

Therefore, we have Q_O hearing impaired, who are able to purchase the hearing aid with their own funds, and $Q_N - Q_O$ hearing impaired, who use standard consumer loans to get aided hearing.

For the $Q_N - Q_O$ hearing impaired, who take a standard consumer loan, the introduction of a subsidized loan for hearing aids purchase will lead to a switch from a standard loan to a subsidized one. In addition, some of the other hearing impaired, who were not able to buy hearing aids without a subsidy for the loan and without a partial lump-sum reimbursement, now will be able to do this. There will be in total Q_L hearing impaired, who are able to afford aided hearing after introduction of subsidized loans. Of them, Q_O will buy hearing aids with their own funds. $Q_N - Q_O$ hearing impaired will switch from a standard consumer loan to a subsidized loan for a hearing aids purchase. Finally, $Q_L - Q_N$ hearing impaired will be able to afford aided hearing with the subsidized loans. This way the subsidy for the loan will have both a substitution and an income effect.

The demand function for subsidized loans is

$$P = \begin{cases} a - bQ, \text{if } Q \leq Q_O \\ a + R_L - b_L Q, \text{if } Q > Q_O \end{cases} \quad (35)$$

where

- Q_O is the quantity of the hearing aids purchased with own funds without a standard consumer loan;
- R_L is the loan subsidy;
- b_L is the slope of the demand curve in the case of a loan subsidy.

Let us assume that the demand curve D_L intersects the supply curve S at the point, which corresponds to the number of the hearing impaired Q_L. Since Q_O hearing impaired buy hearing aids without subsidized loans, the budget of the subsidized loan policy is $(Q_L - Q_O)R_L$. The necessary condition for the subsidized loan policy is the equality of budgets between the partial lump-sum reimbursement policy and the subsidized loan policy.

$$(Q_L - Q_O)R_L = Q_R R \quad (36)$$

where

- Q_L is the quantity of the hearing aids demanded in the case of subsidized loans;
- Q_R is the quantity of the hearing aids demanded in case of partial lump-sum reimbursement.

From the equation (36), we see that $Q_L = Q_O + Q_R \frac{R}{R_L}$. We have assumed above that $R_L < R$. Therefore, $Q_L > Q_R$. Earlier, we have identified that $Q_R > Q_N$. Thus, $Q_L > Q_N$. All this leads us to the conclusion that more hearing impaired are able to afford aided hearing through subsidized loan policy rather than partial lump-sum reimbursement policy or no reimbursement policy at all.

Intuitively, it is also easy to see that although some of the hearing impaired, who originally could afford aided hearing with standard loans, will apply for subsidized loans, others will not do it, because using a subsidized loan to purchase hearing aids effectively increases the price of the hearing aids. If a hearing impaired person has the money available, the lower price is the incentive to avoid using subsidized loans. The hearing impaired, who did not apply for subsidized loans, and purchased hearing aids with their own money, help the payer to allocate more funds for the hearing impaired with lower willingness and ability to pay. This is the main difference from the case of the partial lump-sum reimbursement. Therefore, given the condition of the unchanged policy budget, more hearing impaired are able to afford aided hearing with the help of the subsidized loans policy than with the help of the lump-sum reimbursement policy. Other conditions, which are necessary for this statement to be true are the following:

- The monetary value of the loan subsidy is smaller than the monetary value of the partial lump-sum reimbursement ($R_L < R$);
- There are more than zero people, who buy hearing aids without consumer loans in case no subsidy or reimbursements are available ($Q_O > 0$);
- The $Q_L - Q_O$ hearing impaired are willing and able to take the subsidized loan.

Figure 30 depicts the microeconomic situation of the hearing impaired with subsidized loans. The fat line shows the demand curve D_L – demand for hearing aids in case subsidized loans are available.

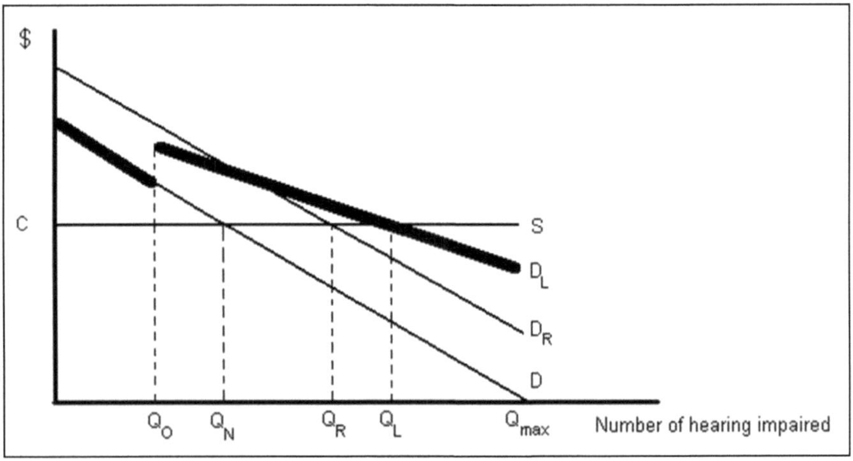

Figure 30: Supply and demand for hearing aids taking into account subsidized loans.[13]

[13] Own illustration using MS Paint 5.1.

Now Q_L hearing impaired people are able to afford aided hearing. However, there are still the hearing impaired who are unable to afford aided hearing even with subsidized loans. These are the hearing impaired, who are not willing or not able to pay the market price C for aided hearing even if subsidized loans are available. The number of them is $Q_{\max} - Q_L$. Neither subsidized loans nor reimbursement within the given budget can help these hearing impaired to afford aided hearing.

One way to help these hearing impaired is to increase the budget for the hearing impairment healthcare policy. We are not exploring this option in this research, because if increasing budget is possible, it makes the solution of the affordability problem very simple. It is more relevant to look for solutions to the affordability problem if increasing the budget is not possible.

Another way is to add the temporal dimension to the problem of affordability of aided hearing. Adding the temporal dimension here means to spend a part of the hearing impairment healthcare policy budget on helping the hearing impaired with the low willingness and ability to get aided hearing later. In other words, the $Q_{\max} - Q_L$ hearing impaired with the lowest willingness and ability to pay should be provided with financial infrastructure and incentives to save. For this purpose, special tax-advantaged savings accounts for healthcare purposes, such as aided hearing, can be used. The assumption on the constant budget to help the hearing impaired remains valid. Therefore, the constant sum of money is now shared among an even larger number of the hearing impaired. Let us assume that in the case of the subsidized savings and loans policy, the subsidy of the same monetary value R_S is given both for savers and for borrowers. We want to help even more people to get access to aided hearing than in the case of the subsidized loans policy. Therefore, the monetary value of the subsidy provided to borrowers in the subsidized savings and loans policy is smaller than the monetary value of the subsidy provided to borrowers in the subsidized loans policy. We can conclude that the subsidy on the loan provided to the hearing impaired decreases from R_L to R_S. Here, $R_S < R_L$. More specifically, given the condition of the unchanged policy budget: $R_S = \dfrac{RQ_R}{Q_{\max} - Q_O}$. The Q_O hearing impaired are able to purchase hearing aids with their own funds without subsidies. They do not take a loan with the R_S subsidy, because this option makes the hearing aid more expensive. They do not have to save money on subsidized savings accounts, as they have enough to buy the hearing aids now. Besides, every rational hearing impaired, who is willing and able to afford aided hearing, wants to get aided hearing sooner, rather than later.

Seeing that the subsidy for the loan is now smaller ($R_S < R_L$), less people are able to afford a bundle of a hearing aid and a subsidized loan. Therefore, the new demand curve for subsidized loans is steeper than D_L, but flatter than D. The intersection of the demand curve for subsidized loans with the subsidy R_S with the supply curve S is at the point Q_F. Please note that the number of the hearing impaired who are able to afford aided hearing through borrowing decreases from Q_L to Q_F, because loan subsidies have decreased. The part of the funds that previously worked for subsidized loans is now used for subsidized savings accounts.

The $Q_F - Q_O$ hearing impaired are able to afford aided hearing through the subsidized loan with the R_S subsidy. We assume that a rational hearing impaired person, who is willing and able to afford aided hearing with the help of a subsidized loan, having a choice between a subsidized savings account and a subsidized loan will choose a subsidized loan, because it allows getting the aided hearing sooner rather than later. The rest $Q_{\max} - Q_F$ hearing impaired get the opportunity to save for aided hearing using subsidized savings account with the subsidy R_S. The $Q_{\max} - Q_F$ hearing impaired with the lowest willingness to pay need to save in order to be able to afford aided hearing, because buying hearing aids from their available funds, or taking a loan is either not possible or not attractive enough for them. Saving up the necessary amount of money will take time, and depending on the personal situation, some might even never be able to save up the necessary sum. Therefore, $Q_{\max} - Q_F$ hearing impaired will not be able to afford aided hearing immediately. This adds the temporal dimension to this problem. The $Q_{\max} - Q_F$ hearing impaired with the lowest willingness to pay are given incentives to save, but it is up to them to take advantage of these incentives. It is also unclear how much time they need to save the sufficient sum to buy the hearing aid.

The aggregate demand curve D_S for the hearing impaired with the subsidized savings and loans healthcare economic policy can be represented with the following equation:

$$P = \begin{cases} a - bQ, if\ Q \le Q_O \\ a + R_S - b_S Q, if\ Q_O < Q \le Q_F \end{cases} \tag{37}$$

where

- Q_F is the quantity of the hearing aids purchased with own funds and subsidized loans in case subsidized loans and savings with the subsidy R_S are available;
- R_S is the loan and savings account subsidy, in case both loan and saving subsidies are present;
- b_S is the slope of the demand curve for subsidized loan in the case both loan and saving subsidies are present.

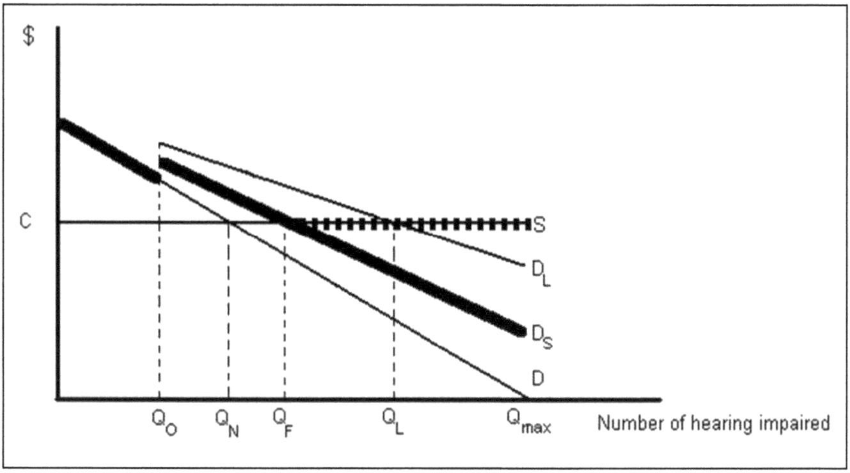

Figure 31: Supply and demand for hearing aids taking into account subsidized loans and savings accounts.[14]

The aggregate demand curve D_S, described in formula (37), shows only the demand that can be immediately fulfilled by the hearing impaired either by paying for the aided hearing completely with their own funds, or by buying hearing aids with the help of the subsidized loan. Since $Q_L < Q_F$, fewer hearing impaired are able to afford hearing aids immediately with the help of the subsidized savings and loans policy than with the help of the subsidized loans policy. The $Q_{\max} - Q_F$ hearing impaired with the lowest willingness to pay are offered incentives to save for the purchase of the hearing aid later. Therefore, although it is theoretically possible that all remaining hearing impaired will take subsidized savings accounts and eventually buy hearing aids, it is not certain what percentage of the $Q_{\max} - Q_F$ hearing impaired with the lowest willingness to pay will eventually be able to save enough money and afford aided hearing.

Figure 31 depicts the microeconomic situation of the hearing impaired with subsidized savings and loans. The fat line shows the demand curve D_S – demand for aided hearing in case subsidized savings and loans are available. The dotted fat line shows that the $Q_{\max} - Q_F$ hearing impaired with the lowest willingness to pay may eventually afford aided hearing with the help of the saving subsidy R_S.

The subsidized savings and loans healthcare economic policy gives an opportunity for all hearing impaired in the population eventually to get access to aided hearing. The Q_O of the hearing impaired with the highest willingness and ability to pay can finance their aided hearing from their own funds, the next

[14] Own illustration using MS Paint 5.1.

$Q_F - Q_O$ hearing impaired can afford aided hearing through subsidized loans with the R_S subsidy, and the $Q_{\max} - Q_F$ with the lowest willingness to pay can save for their aided hearing on subsidized savings accounts with the R_S subsidy. The advantage of the subsidized savings and loans healthcare economic policy over the partial reimbursement healthcare economic policy is that in the former the hearing impaired with the highest willingness to pay are not over-reimbursed. Instead these funds are used to help the hearing impaired who are not able to afford aided hearing without subsidies.

A subsidized savings and loans policy opens the way for all hearing impaired willing to get a hearing aid to afford one. The disadvantage of this policy is that many hearing impaired will have to wait until they save up enough money before they can buy a hearing aid. Besides, the hearing impaired without any income are not able to contribute to the savings account, and thus they might either never save enough to afford aided hearing or might have to wait quite long before they get access to aided hearing. On the other hand, the subsidized loans policy allows more hearing impaired to afford aided hearing immediately compared to the subsidized saving and loans policy, or the partial lump-sum reimbursement policy. The disadvantage of the subsidized loans policy over the subsidized savings and loans policy is that the subsidized loans policy does not provide incentives to the hearing impaired with the lowest willingness to pay to save up and afford a hearing aid. The subsidized savings and loans policy achieves this with the help of the subsidized loans.

7 Conclusion

Hearing impairment is a complex disability. Its impact on quality of life can vary greatly depending on the type and degree of hearing loss. Without any doubts, full reimbursement of hearing aids for all hearing impaired around the globe is the most humane solution. Unfortunately, it is very costly and only some of the richest societies in the world can afford it. Most countries often deal with the limited healthcare budget, which they prefer to use cost-effectively. This research shows that willingness to integrate into the hearing society, and willingness and ability to finance the purchase of a hearing instrument or an implant are key factors behind successful social inclusion of the hearing impaired. There are multiple ways to finance the purchase of hearing instruments or implants, but each of them consists of certain components of borrowing and saving.

Our research shows that the subsidized loans healthcare economic policy for hearing impairment is more cost-effective than the partial lump-sum reimbursement policy currently implemented in Russia and other countries. Besides, we show that the subsidized savings and loans policy doesn't have the demerits of under- and overreimbursement that partial reimbursement policy has. The subsidized loans policy gives an opportunity for bigger number of hearing impaired to afford a hearing aid than the partial lump-sum reimbursement policy does. Future research could prove this statement also by building a Markov Model and comparing the outcomes of both policies in QALY, while keeping the budget constant for both policies. For this research, we used data on the hearing impaired mostly from Russia and Ukraine, but the recommendations of this research can also be applicable to other countries.

Furthermore, it is essential to test the theory in practice. The goal of such tests should be to get the feedback on the actual implementation of the proposed subsidized loans and subsidized savings and loans healthcare economic policies. It remains to be defined how exactly the subsidized aided hearing savings accounts and subsidized loans will be implemented practically. It depends on the existing legal framework in the given country, availability of consumer banking, microfinance institutions and economic stability. It could be especially challenging in the developing countries, where income levels are very low and financial infrastructure is undeveloped. Due to the non-zero operating costs of using hearing instruments and implants, such as cost of batteries, aided hearing might not work for the poorest.

Consequently, this study calls for more research in order to analyze the ability to pay back loans by the hearing impaired, ways to make subsidized savings and loans available for the hearing impaired, and assess the satisfaction with the aided hearing of the hearing impaired. Only a broad and well-financed field project can answer the question whether the theory developed in this research can help increase quality of life of the hearing impaired.

References

Abrams, H., Hnath-Chisolm, T., Guerreeiro, S., & Ritterman, S. (1992). The effect of intervention strategy on self-perception of hearing handicap. *Ear and Hearing*, 13(5), 371-377.

Abrahamson, J. (1997). Patient education and peer interaction facilitate hearing aid adjustment. *The Hearing Review*, 4(1),19-22.

AHIP Center for Policy and Research (2008). *Health Savings Accounts and Account-Based Health Plans: Research Highlights*. Retrived January 27, 2013, from http://www.ahip.org/Issues/Documents/2011/Health-Savings-Accounts-and-Account-Based-Health-Plans--Research-Highlights.aspx

Armendariz de Aghion, B., & Morduch, J. (2000). Microfinance Beyond Group Lending. *Economics of Transition,* 8 (2), 401-420.

Ashraf, N., Karlan D. & Yin, W. (2006). Tying Odysseus to the Mast: Evidence from a Commitment Savings Product in the Philippines. *Quarterly Journal of Economics*, 121(2), 673-697.

Beverly, S., Moore, A., & Schreiner, M. (2003). A Framework of Asset Accumulation Stages and Strategies. *Journal of Family and Economic Issues*, 24(2),143-156.

Beverly, S., & Sherraden, M. (1999) Institutional determinants of savings: implications for low-income households and public policy, *Journal of Socio-Economics*, 28, 457-473.

Bhole, B., & Ogden, S. (2010). Group lending and individual lending with strategic default. *Journal of Development Economics*, 91, 348-363.

Bollen, K. (1989). *Structural Equations with Latent Variables*. New York, USA: Wiley & Sons.

Bollen, K. (1987), Outliers and improper solutions: A confirmatory factor analysis example. *Sociological Methods and Research*, 15, 375–384.

Bosman, A., Snik, A., Mylanus, E., & Cremers, C. (2006). Fitting range of the BAHA Cordelle. *International Journal of Audiology,* 45(8), 429-37.

Boutayeb, A. (2006). Social inequalities and health inequity in Morocco. *International Journal for Equity in Health*, 5, 1-6.

Brooks, D. (1990). Measures for the assessment of hearing aid provision and rehabilitation. British Journal of Audiology, 24(4), 229-233.

Brown, T. (2006). *Confirmatory Factor Analysis for Applied Research*. New York, USA: Guilford Press.

Browne, M. (1984). Asymptotic distribution free methods in the analysis of covariance structures. *British Journal of Mathematical and Statistical Psychology*, 37, 62-83.

Burstrom, K., Johannesson, M., & Diderichsen, F. (2006). A comparison of individual and social time trade-off values for health states in the general population. *Health Policy*, 76(3), 359-370.

Byrne, B. (1994). *Structural Equation Modeling with EQS and EQS/Windows: Basic Concepts, Applications, and Programming*. Thousand Oaks, USA: Sage Publications.

Carmines, E., & McIver, J. (1981). Analyzing Models with Unobserved Variables: Analysis of Covariance Structures. In G. W. Bohrnstedt & E. F. Borgatta (Eds.), *Social Measurement: Current Issues* (pp. 65-115). Beverly Hills, USA: Sage Publications.

Cheng, A., & Niparko, J. (1999). Cost-utility of the cochlear implant in adults. *Archives of Otolaryngology - Head and Neck Surgery*, 125(11), 1214-1218.

Ching, T., Dillon, H., & Byrne, D. (1998). Speech recognition of hearing-impaired listeners: Predictions from audibility and the limited role of high-frequency amplification. *Journal of the Acoustical Society of America*, 103(2), 1128–1140.

Ching, T., Dillon, H., Katsch, R. & Byrne, D. (2001). Maximizing effective audibility in hearing aid fitting. *Ear and Hearing*, 22(3), 212–224.

Chou, C., & Bentler, P. (1995). Estimates and tests in structural equation modeling. In R. H. Hoyle (Ed.), *Structural equation modeling: Concepts, issues, and applications* (pp. 37-55). Thousand Oaks, USA: Sage Publications.

Clarke, M., Bailie, K., Connolly, S., & Murray, L. (2013). Clinical epidemiology and evidence-based practice. In J. Yarnell & D. O'Reilly (Eds.), Epidemiology and Disease Prevention (pp. 66-86). Oxford, UK: Oxford University Press.

Collins, D., Morduch, J., Rutherford, S., & Ruthven, O. (2009). *Portfolios of the Poor: How the World's Poor Live on $2 a Day*. Princeton, USA: Princeton University Press.

Conning, J. (2000). *Monitoring by delegates or by peers? Joint liability loans under moral hazard*. Working Paper, Williams College Center of Development Economics. Retrieved from http://web.williams.edu/Economics/wp/jliability.pdf

Cox, R. & Alexander, G. (1999). Measuring Satisfaction with Amplification in Daily Life: the SADL scale. *Ear and Hearing*, 20(4), 306-320.

Cox, R. & Alexander, G. (2002). The International Outcome Inventory for Hearing Aids (IOI-HA): psychometric properties of the English version. *International Journal of Audiology*, 41(1), 30-35.

Cox, R., Hyde, M., Gatehouse, S., Noble, W., Dillon, H., Bentler, R., Stephens, D., Arlinger, S., Beck, L., Wilkerson, D., Kramer, S., Kricos, P., Gagne, J., Bess, F., & Hallberg, L. (2000). Optimal outcome measures, research priorities, and international cooperation. *Ear and Hearing*, 21(4), 106S-115S.

Daher, H., & Flessa, S. (2010). Microfinance as a tool for financing medical devices in Syria. An assessment of needs and a call for further research. *Journal of Public Health*, 18, 189-197.

Del Dot, J., Hickson, L., & O'Connel, B. (1992). Speech perception in noise with BiCROS hearing aids. *Scandinavian Audiology*, 21(4), 261-264.

Denzin, N., & Lincoln, Y. (1994). *Computer-aided qualitative data analysis*. Thousand Oaks, USA: Sage Publications.

Denzin, N., & Lincoln, Y. (2005). *The Sage Handbook of qualitative research. Third Edition*. Thousand Oaks, USA: Sage Publications.

Dillon, H (2001). *Hearing Aids*. Tarramurra, Australia: Boomerang Press.

Dillon, W., Kumar, A., & Mulani, N. (1987). Offending estimates in covariance structure analysis: Comments on the causes of and solutions to Heywood cases. *Psychological Bulletin*, 101(1), 126-135.

Dolan, P., Gudex, C., Kind, P., Williams, A. (1996a). The time trade-off method: results from a general population study. *Health Economics*, 5(2), 141–154.

Dolan, P., Gudex, C., Kind, P., & Williams, A. (1996b). Valuing health states: a comparison of methods. *Journal of Health Economics*, 15(2), 209–231.

Dupas, P., & Robinson, J. (2013). Why Don't the Poor Save More? Evidence from Health Savings Experiments. *The American Economic Review*, 103(4), 1138-1171.

Erdman, S., Crowley, J., & Gillespie, G. (1984). Considerations in counseling for the hearing impaired. *Hearing Instruments*, 35(11), 50-58.

Friedman, M. (1957). *A Theory of the Consumption Function*. Princeton, USA: Princeton University Press.

Gatehouse, S. (1999). Glasgow Hearing Aid Benefit Profile: derivation and validation of a client-centered outcome measure for hearing aid services. *Journal of the American Academy of Audiology*, 10(2), 80-103.

Giné, X., & Karlan, D. (2011) *Group versus Individual Liability: Short and Long Term Evidence from Philippine Microcredit Lending Groups*. Working Paper, Yale University. Retrieved from http://karlan.yale.edu/p/GroupversusIndividualLending.pdf.

Ghatak, M. (1999). Group lending, local information and peer selection. *Journal of Development Economics*, 60(1), 27-50.

Ghatak, M., & Guinnane, T. (1999). The Economics of Lending with Joint Liability: Theory and Practice. *Journal of Development Economics*, 60(1), 95-229.

Ghatak, M. (2000). Screening by the company you keep: Joint liability lending and the peer selection effect. *The Economic Journal*, 110, 601-631.

Glaser, B., & Strauss, A. (1967). *The discovery of grounded theory: Strategies for qualitative research*. Chicago, USA: Aldine Publishing Company.

Glied, S., & Remler., D. (2005). The Effect of Health Savings Accounts on Health Insurance Coverage. *Issue Brief (The Commonwealth Fund)*, April (811), 1-8.

Gold, M., Siegel, J., Russel, U., Weinstein, M. (1996). *Cost-Effectiveness in Health and Medicine*. New York, USA: Oxford University Press.

Goodman, J. (2006). *Statement on Health Savings Accounts*. Testimony Before the U.S. Senate Finance Committee Subcommittee on Health Care. Retrieved from http://www.ncpa.org/speech/statement-on-health-savings-accounts

Handicap International (2006). *Good Practices for the Economic Inclusion of People with Disabilities in Developing Countries*. Lyon, France: Handicap International.

Hakansson, B., Tjellström, A., Rosenhall, U., & Carlsson, P. (1985). The bone-anchored hearing aid. Principal design and a psychoacoustical evaluation. *Acta oto-laryngoogica,* 100(3-4),229-239.

Harrington, D. (2009). *Confirmatory factor analysis. (Pocket Guides to Social Work Research Methods)*. New York, USA: Oxford University Press.

Hickson, L., Hamilton, L., & Orange, S. (1986). Factors associated with hearing aid use. *Australian Journal of Audiology*, 8(2),37-41.

Hickson, L., Timm, M., Worrall, L., & Bishop, K. (1999). Hearing aid fitting: outcomes for older adults. *Australian Journal of Audiology*, 21(1),9-21.

Hogan, A., Taylor, A., Doyle, J., Osborn, R., Fitzmaurice, K., & Kendig, H. (2001). The communication and health needs of older people with hearing loss: are hearing aids enough? *Australian and New Zealand Journal of Audiology*, 23(1),10-17.

Hougaard S. & Ruf, S. (2010). *EuroTrak: New survey of the market for hearing aids in Germany, France and the U.K. First globally comparative study of hearing, hearing loss and hearing aids*, Retrieved from http://www.ehima.com/ehima2/euha_eurotrak_oct_2010_final.pdf

Hu, L., & Bentler, P. (1995). Evaluating model fit. In R. H. Hoyle (Ed.), *Structural equation modeling: Concepts, issues, and applications* (pp. 76 –99). Thousand Oaks, USA: Sage Publications.

Jespersen, C., Groth, J., Kiessling, J., Brenner, B., & Jensen, O. (2006). The occlusion effect in unilateral versus bilateral hearing aids. *Journal of the American Academy of Audiology*; 17(10), 763-73.

Joore, M., Brunenberg, D., Chenault, M., & Anteunis, L. (2003). Societal effects of hearing aid fitting among the moderately hearing impaired. *International Journal of Audiology*, 42(3), 152-160.

Jöreskog, K. G. (1970). A general method for analysis of covariance structures. *Biometrika*, 57(2), 239–251.

Jöreskog, K. & Sörbom, D. (1996). *LISREL 8: User's Reference Guide*. Chicago, USA: Scientific Software International Inc.

Kaplan, D. (2000).*Structural equation modeling: Foundations and extensions*. Thousand Oaks, USA: Sage Publications.

Karlan, D., & Zinman, J. (2005). *Elasticities of demand for consumer credit*. New Haven, USA: Yale University, Economic Growth Center.

Keren, R., Helfand, M., Homer, C., McPhillips, H., & Lieu, T. (2002). Projected cost-effectiveness of statewide universal newborn hearing screening. *Pediatrics*, 110(5), 855–895.

Kiessling, J. (2008). Versorgung mit Hörgeräten. In: J. Kiessling, B. Kollmeier, & G. Diller (Eds.), *Versorgung und Rehabilitation mit Hörgeräten* (pp. 59-130). Stuttgart, Germany: Thieme Verlag.

Kiessling, J., Brenner, B., Jespersen, C., Groth, J., & Jensen, O. (2005). Occlusion effect of earmolds with different venting systems. *Journal of American Academy of Audiology*, 16(4), 237-249.

Kline, R. (2011). *Principles and practice of structural equation modeling*. New York, USA: Guilford Press.

Kochkin, S. (1993). MarkeTrak III: Higher hearing aid sales don't signal better market penetration. *The Hearing Journal*, 46 (7), 47-54.

Kochkin, S. (2005). *The Impact of Untreated Hearing Loss on Household Income.* Better Hearing Institute. Retrieved from http://www.hearing.org/uploadedFiles/Content/impact_of_untreated_hearing_loss_on_income.pdf

Kochkin, S. (2007). Marke Trak VII: Obstacles to adult non-user adoption of hearing aids. *The Hearing Journal*, 60(4), 24-51.

Kochkin, S. (2010). Marke Trak VIII: The efficacy of hearing aids in achieving compensation equity in the workplace. *The Hearing Journal*, 63(10), 19-26.

Kochkin, S. (2013). *The Impact of Treated Hearing Loss on Quality of Life.* Better Hearing Institute. Retrieved from http://www.betterhearing.org/aural_education_and_counseling/articles_tip_sheets_and_guides/hearing_loss_treatment/quality_of_life.pdf

Kochkin, S., & Rogin, C. (2000). Quantifying the obvious: the impact of hearing aids on quality of life. *The Hearing Review,* 7(1), 8-34.

Laibson, D. (1997). Golden Eggs and Hyperbolic Discounting. *The Quarterly Journal of Economics*, 112(2), 443-478.

Lenarz, T., Lim, H., Reuter, G., Patrick J., & Lenarz, M (2006). The auditory midbrain implant: a new auditory prosthesis for neural deafness - concept and device description. *Otology & Neurotology: official publication of the American Otological Society, American Neurotology Society, and European Academy of Otology and Neurotology*, 27(6), 838-843.

Lewis, C. (2004). Microfinance from the point of view of women with disabilities: lessons from Zambia and Zimbabwe. *Gender and Development*, 12(1), 28-39.

Lin F., Metter E., O'Brien R., Resnick S., Zonderman A., Ferrucci L. (2011). Hearing loss and incident dementia. *Archives of Neurology*, 68(2), 214-220.

Lowenstein, G., & Thaler, R. (1989). Anomalies: Intertemporal Choice. *Journal of Economic Perspectives*, 3(4),181-193.

Luetje, C., Thedinger, B., Buckler, L., Dawson, K., & Lisbona, K. (2007). Hybrid cochlear implantation: clinical results and critical review in 13 cases. *Otology & Neurotology: official publication of the American Otological Society, American Neurotology Society, and European Academy of Otology and Neurotology*, 28(4), 473-478.

Lusardi, A. (2001). *Explaining Why So Many Households Do Not Save.* Working Paper, Dartmouth College. Retrieved from http://crr.bc.edu/wp-content/uploads/2001/09/wp_2001-05.pdf

Macrae, J., & Dillon H. (1996). Gain, frequency response and maximum output requirements for hearing aids. *J Rehab Res Dev*, 33(4), 363-376.

Maital, S. (1986). Prometheus Rebound: On Welfare-Improving Constraints. *Eastern Economic Journal*, 12(3), 337-344.

Manning, W., Newhouse, J., Duan, N., Keeler, E., Leibowitz, A., & Marquis, S. (1987). Health Insurance and the Demand for Medical Care: Evidence from a Randomized Experiment. *The American Economic Review*, 77(3), 251-277.

Martin, A., Glasziou, P., Simes, R., & Lumley, T. (2000). A comparison of standard gamble, time trade-off, and adjusted time trade-off scores. *International Journal of Technology Assessment in Health Care*, 16(1), 137–147.

Mathers, C., Smith, A., & Concha, M. (2003). *Global Burden of Hearing Loss in the Year 2000*, Working Paper, World Health Organization. Retrived from http://www.who.int/healthinfo/statistics/bod_hearingloss.pdf

Matisson, S. (2002). *Medical Savings Accounts and Prescription Drugs: Evidence from South Africa.* NCPA Policy Report Report No. 254, The National Center for Policy Analysis. Retrieved from http://www.ncpa.org/pub/st254

Mersland, R. (2005). *Microcredit for Self-employed Disabled Persons in Developing Countries*. Oslo, Norway: Atlas Alliance.

Ministry of Health Care and Social Development of Russian Federation (2011) *Об Утверждении порядка выплаты компенсации за самостоятельно приобретенное инвалидом техническое средство реабилитации и (или) оказанную услугу, включая порядок определения ее размера и порядок информирования граждан о размере указанной компенсации. Приказ от 31 января 2011 г. N 57н.* Retrieved from http://r41.fss.ru/31291/42749/index.shtml

Mitchell, P. (2002). *The Prevalence, Risk Factors and Impacts of Hearing Impairment in an Older Australian Community: The Blue Mountains Hearing Survey. The 4th Issue of Libby Harricks Memorial Oration*. Braddon, Australia: Deafness Forum.

Moeller, J., Schmidt, C., & Lasser, C. (2004). Gesundheit der Ökonomie und Ökonomie der Gesundheit: Eine kritische Auseinandersetzung mit dem WHO-Bericht „Macroeconomics and Health". *Journal of Public Health*, 12(1), 3-9.

Modigliani, F. (1966). The life-cycle hypothesis of saving, the demand for wealth, and the supply of capital. *Social Research*, 33(1), 160-217.

Mohr, P., Feldman, J., Dunbar, J., McConkey-Robbins, A., Niparko, J., Rittenhouse, R., & Skinner, M. (2000). The societal costs of severe to profound hearing loss in the United States. *International Journal of Technology Assessment in Health Care*, 16(4), 1120-1135.

Mulaik, S., James, L., Van Alstine, J., Bennet, N., Lind, S., & Stilwell, C. (1989), Evaluation of Goodness-of-Fit Indices for Structural Equation Models, *Psychological Bulletin*, 105 (3), 430-45.

Niparko, J. (2009). *Cochlear implants: principles & practices*, Philadelphia, USA: Lippincott Williams and Wilkins.

O'Donahue, T., & Rabin, M., (1999). Doing it Now or Doing it Later.*The American Economic Review*, 89(1),103-121.

Ozanna, L. (1996). How will medical savings accounts affect medical spending? *Inquiry*, 33, 225-236.

Preedy, V., & Watson, R. (2009) *Handbook of Disease Burdens and Quality of Life Measures*. New York, USA: Springer.

Rai, A., & Sjöström, T., (2004). Is Grameen Lending Efficient? Repayment Incentives and Insurance in Village Economies.*Review of Economic Studies*, 71, 217-234.

Reiter, R., Pickhard, A., & Brosch, S. (2012). Periphere Hörstörungen und Spracherwerb. *Laryngorhinootologie*, 91(9), 550-559.

Rindskopf, D. (1984). Structural equation models: Empirical identification, Heywood cases, and related problems, *Sociological Methods and Research*, 13(1), 109–119.

Rosahl, S., Lenarz, T., Matthies, C., Samii, M., Sollmann, W., & Laszig, R. (2004). Hirnstammimplantante zur Wiederherstellung des Hörvermögens – Entwicklung und Perspektiven. *Deutsches Ärtzeblatt*, 101(4), A180-A188

Rottenberg, S. (1990). Unintended Consequences: The Probable Effects of Mandated Medical Insurance. *Regulation*, 13, 27-28.

Ruben, R. (2001). Redefining the survival of the fittest: communication disorders in the 21st century. *Laryngoscope*, 111(6), 1115-1116.

Schreyögg, J. (2003). Medical Savings Accounts - Eine internationale Bestandsaufnahme des Konzeptes der Gesundheitssparkonten und seine Implikationen für Deutschland. *Zeitschrift für die gesamte Versicherungswissenschaft*, 92(3), 507-532.

Shefrin, H., & Thaler, R. (1988). The Behavioral Life-Cycle Hypothesis. *Economic Inquiry*, 26(4), 609-643.

Snik, A., Bosman, A., Mylanus, E., & Cremers, C. (2004). Candidacy for the bone-anchored hearing aid. *Audiology and Neurootology*, 9(4), 190-196.

Snik, A., Mylanus, E., Proops, D., Wolfaard, J., Hodgetts, W., Somers, T., Niparko, J., Wazen J., Sterkers, O., Cremers, C., & Tjellström, A. (2005). Consensus statements on the BAHA system: where do we stand at present? *The Annals of Otology, Rhinology and Laryngology. Supplement*,195, 2-12.

Stenfelt, S. (2005) Bilateral fitting of BAHAs and BAHA fitted in unilateral deaf persons: acoustical aspects. *International Journal of Audiology*, 44(3), 178-189.

Stephens, D., & Kerr, P. (2000). Auditory disablements: an update. *Audiology: official organ of the International Society of Audiology*, 39(6), 322-332.

Stiglitz, J., & Weiss, A. (1981). Credit rationing in markets with imperfect information. *The American Economic Review*, 71(3), 393-410.

Stiglitz, J. (1990). Peer Monitoring and Credit Markets. *The World Bank Economic Review*, 4(3), 351-366.

Strauss, A., & Corbin, J. (1998). Grounded theory methodology: An overview. In N. K. Denzin & Y. S. Lincoln (Eds.), *Strategies of qualitative inquiry* (pp. 158–183). Thousand Oaks, USA: Sage Publications.

Suhrcke, M., McKee, M., Arce, R., Tsolova, S., & Mortensen, J. (2005). *The contribution of health to the economy in the European Union*. Luxemburg, Luxemburg: European Commission.

Summerfield, A., Marshall, D., Barton, G., & Bloor, K.. (2002). A cost-utility scenario analysis of bilateral cochlear implantation. *Archives of Otolaryngology - Head and Neck Surgery*, 128(11), 1255-1262.

Thaler, R. (1990). Anomalies: Saving, Fungibility and Mental Accounts. *The Journal of Economic Perspectives*, 4(1), 193-205.

Thaler, R. (1994). Psychology and Savings Policies. *The American Economic Review*, 84(2), 186-192.

Thaler, R., & Shefrin, H. (1981). An Economic Theory of Self-Control. *Journal of Political Economy*, 89(2), 392-406.

Tjellström, A., Hakansson, B., & Granstrom, G. (2001). Bone-anchored hearing aids: current status in adults and children. *Otolaryngologic Clinics of North America*, 34(2), 337-64.

Van Maanen, J. (1998). *Qualitative studies of organizations*. Thousand Oaks, USA: Sage Publications.

Voogdt, U. (2005). *Otoplastik. Die individuelle Otoplastik zur Hörgeräte-Versorgung und als persönlicher Gehörschutz im Lärm*. Heidelberg, Germany: Median-Verlag.

Wazen, J., Spitzer, J., Ghossaini, S., Fayad, J., Niparko, J., Cox, K., Brackmann, D., & Soli, S. (2003). Transcranial contralateral cochlear stimulation in unilateral deafness. *Otolaryngology - Head and Neck Surgery*, 129(3), 248-254.

West, S., Finch, J., & Curran, P. (1995). Structural equation models with nonnormal variables: Problems and remedies. In R. Hoyle (Ed.), *Structural equation modeling: Concepts, issues, and applications* (pp. 56-75). Thousand Oaks, USA: Sage Publications.

Williams, I., Robinson, S., & Dickinson, H. (2012). *Rationing in health care: the theory and practice of priority setting*. Bristol, UK: The Policy Press.

Wilson, D., Xibin, S., Read, P., Walsh, P., & Esterman, A. (1992). Hearing loss – an underestimated public health problem, *Australian Journal of Public Health*, 16(3), 282-286.

Wolfensohn, J. (2002, December 3). Poor, Disabled and Shut Out. The Washington Post. Retrieved from http://bvs.per.paho.org/texcom/cd048370/disabled.pdf

Wong, B., Hui, Y., Au, D., and Wei, W. (2000) Economic evaluation of cochlear implantation. *Advances in Oto-Rhino-Laryngology*, 57, 377–381.

World Health Organization. (1980). *International Classification of Impairments, Disabilities and Handicaps*. Retrieved from http://whqlibdoc.who.int/publications/1980/9241541261_eng.pdf

World Health Organization. (1991) *Report of the Informal Working Group On Prevention Of Deafness And Hearing*. Retrieved from http://whqlibdoc.who.int/hq/1991/WHO_PDH_91.1.pdf

World Health Organization. (2001). *Macroeconomics and Health: Investing in Health for Economic Development. Report of the commission on macroeconomics and health*. Retrieved from http://whqlibdoc.who.int/publications/2001/924154550x.pdf

World Health Organization. (2013). *Deafness and Hearing Impairment. Fact Sheet N. 300*. Retrieved from http://www.who.int/mediacentre/factsheets/fs300/en/

Appendix

A-1: Questionnaire for People with Hearing Loss

Questionnaire for people with hearing loss

Hearing loss and hearing aid in the right ear

Data collection on the hearing loss and hearing aids in the right ear

1. Describe your hearing in the right ear without use of a hearing instrument or prior to implantation

◯ No hearing loss. I have no difficulty in speech understanding

◯ Mild hearing loss. I may have difficulty understanding very quite speech in noise, or distant speech

◯ Moderate hearing loss. I understand conversation only at a distance of no more than 10 feet. In background noise I don't comprehend up to 50% of speech

◯ Severe hearing loss. Conversation must be very loud to be heard without amplification. I am aware of loud voices about one foot from the ear without amplification but most likely to rely on vision for communication

◯ Deafness

2. Enter your air conduction audiogram for the right ear if you remember it

	125 Hz	250 Hz	500 Hz	750 Hz	1000 Hz	1500 Hz	2000 Hz	3000 Hz	4000 Hz	6000 Hz	8000 Hz
0 dB	☐	☐	☐	☐	☐	☐	☐	☐	☐	☐	☐
10 dB	☐	☐	☐	☐	☐	☐	☐	☐	☐	☐	☐
20 dB	☐	☐	☐	☐	☐	☐	☐	☐	☐	☐	☐
30 dB	☐	☐	☐	☐	☐	☐	☐	☐	☐	☐	☐
40 dB	☐	☐	☐	☐	☐	☐	☐	☐	☐	☐	☐
50 dB	☐	☐	☐	☐	☐	☐	☐	☐	☐	☐	☐
60 dB	☐	☐	☐	☐	☐	☐	☐	☐	☐	☐	☐
70 dB	☐	☐	☐	☐	☐	☐	☐	☐	☐	☐	☐
80 dB	☐	☐	☐	☐	☐	☐	☐	☐	☐	☐	☐
90 dB	☐	☐	☐	☐	☐	☐	☐	☐	☐	☐	☐
100 dB	☐	☐	☐	☐	☐	☐	☐	☐	☐	☐	☐
110 dB	☐	☐	☐	☐	☐	☐	☐	☐	☐	☐	☐
120 dB	☐	☐	☐	☐	☐	☐	☐	☐	☐	☐	☐

Questionnaire for people with hearing loss

3. Which type of hearing aid do you use in your right ear?

- ◯ Sound amplifier or assistive listening device
- ◯ Pocket hearing aid
- ◯ Invisible-in-Canal (IIC)
- ◯ Completely-in-the-canal (CIC)
- ◯ Mini-Canal (MC)
- ◯ In-the-canal (ITC)
- ◯ Half-Shell (HS)
- ◯ In-the-ear full concha Instrument (ST or Concha)
- ◯ Behind-the-ear (BTE)
- ◯ Over-the-ear (OTE)
- ◯ Small BTE instrument with Receiver-in-canal (RIC)
- ◯ Cros/Bicros
- ◯ Middle ear implant
- ◯ Bone anchored hearing aid (BAHA)
- ◯ Cochlear Implant (CI)
- ◯ Auditory Brainstem Implant (ABI)
- ◯ Other type of hearing aid
- ◯ I have no hearing aid in my right ear

4. Where did you buy your hearing aid for the right ear?

- ◯ Via hearing aid dispenser, ENT doctor, audiologist, otolaryngologist, or any other expert in hearing instruments
- ◯ Via internet, without any help from a specialist in hearing instruments
- ◯ In some other place, without any help from a specialist in hearing instruments
- ◯ I have an implant in my right ear
- ◯ I have neither a hearing instrument nor an implant in my right ear

5. What kind of technology does the hearing instrument in your right ear have?

- ◯ Analog hearing instrument
- ◯ Trimmer digital hearing instrument
- ◯ Digital computer-programmable hearing instrument
- ◯ I don't know the type of the hearing instrument in my right ear
- ◯ I have an implant in my right ear
- ◯ I have neither a hearing instrument nor an implant in my right ear

Questionnaire for people with hearing loss

6. Are you happy with your hearing instrument or implant in the right ear?

- ◯ Yes
- ◯ Rather yes, than no
- ◯ Undecided
- ◯ Rather no, than yes
- ◯ No
- ◯ I have neither a hearing instrument nor an implant in my right ear

7. Enter the make and model of your hearing instrument or implant sound processor in the right ear

[ ]

8. How long do you use your current hearing aid in your right ear?

- ◯ Less than 6 weeks
- ◯ 6 weeks to 11 months
- ◯ 1 year to 10 years
- ◯ Over 10 years
- ◯ I have no hearing aid in my right ear

9. What is your total experience with the hearing aids, including all hearing instruments and implants that you ever had, in your right ear?

- ◯ Less than 6 weeks
- ◯ 6 weeks to 11 months
- ◯ 1 year to 10 years
- ◯ Over 10 years
- ◯ I have never had any hearing aid in my right ear

Questionnaire for people with hearing loss

Hearing loss and hearing aid in the left ear

Data collection on the hearing loss and hearing aids in the left ear

10. Describe your hearing in the left ear without use of a hearing instrument or prior to implantation

◯ No hearing loss. I have no difficulty in speech understanding

◯ Mild hearing loss. I may have difficulty understanding very quite speech in noise, or distant speech

◯ Moderate hearing loss. I understand conversation only at distance no more than 10 feet. In background noise I don't perceive up to 50% of speech

◯ Severe hearing loss. Conversation must be very loud to be heard without amplification. I am aware of loud voices about one foot from the ear without amplification but most likely to rely on vision for communication

◯ Deafness

11. Enter your air conduction audiogram for the left ear if you remember it

	125 Hz	250 Hz	500 Hz	750 Hz	1000 Hz	1500 Hz	2000 Hz	3000 Hz	4000 Hz	6000 Hz	8000 Hz
0 dB	☐	☐	☐	☐	☐	☐	☐	☐	☐	☐	☐
10 dB	☐	☐	☐	☐	☐	☐	☐	☐	☐	☐	☐
20 dB	☐	☐	☐	☐	☐	☐	☐	☐	☐	☐	☐
30 dB	☐	☐	☐	☐	☐	☐	☐	☐	☐	☐	☐
40 dB	☐	☐	☐	☐	☐	☐	☐	☐	☐	☐	☐
50 dB	☐	☐	☐	☐	☐	☐	☐	☐	☐	☐	☐
60 dB	☐	☐	☐	☐	☐	☐	☐	☐	☐	☐	☐
70 dB	☐	☐	☐	☐	☐	☐	☐	☐	☐	☐	☐
80 dB	☐	☐	☐	☐	☐	☐	☐	☐	☐	☐	☐
90 dB	☐	☐	☐	☐	☐	☐	☐	☐	☐	☐	☐
100 dB	☐	☐	☐	☐	☐	☐	☐	☐	☐	☐	☐
110 dB	☐	☐	☐	☐	☐	☐	☐	☐	☐	☐	☐
120 dB	☐	☐	☐	☐	☐	☐	☐	☐	☐	☐	☐

Questionnaire for people with hearing loss

12. Which type of hearing aid do you use in your left ear?

- ◯ Sound amplifier or assistive listening device
- ◯ Pocket hearing aid
- ◯ Invisible-in-Canal (IIC)
- ◯ Completely-in-the-canal (CIC)
- ◯ Mini-Canal (MC)
- ◯ In-the-canal (ITC)
- ◯ Half-Shell (HS)
- ◯ In-the-ear full concha Instrument (ST or concha)
- ◯ Behind-the-ear (BTE)
- ◯ Over-the-ear (OTE)
- ◯ Small BTE instrument with Receiver-in-canal (RIC)
- ◯ Cros/Bicros
- ◯ Middle ear implant
- ◯ Bone anchored hearing aid (BAHA)
- ◯ Cochlear Implant (CI)
- ◯ Auditory Brainstem Implant (ABI)
- ◯ Other type of hearing aid
- ◯ I have no hearing aid in my left ear

13. Where did you buy your hearing aid for the left ear?

- ◯ Via hearing aid dispenser, ENT doctor, audiologist, otolaryngologist, or any other expert in hearing instruments
- ◯ Via internet, without any help from a specialist in hearing instruments
- ◯ In some other place, without any help from a specialist in hearing instruments
- ◯ I have an implant in my left ear
- ◯ I have neither a hearing instrument nor an implant in my left ear

14. What kind of technology does the hearing instrument in your left ear have?

- ◯ Analog hearing instrument
- ◯ Trimmer digital hearing instrument
- ◯ Digital computer-programmable hearing instrument
- ◯ I don't know the type of the hearing instrument in my left ear
- ◯ I have an implant in my left ear
- ◯ I have neither a hearing instrument nor an implant in my left ear

Questionnaire for people with hearing loss

15. Are you happy with your hearing instrument or implant in the left ear?

- ◯ Yes
- ◯ Rather yes, than no
- ◯ Undecided
- ◯ Rather no, than yes
- ◯ No
- ◯ I have neither a hearing instrument nor an implant in my left ear

16. Enter the make and model of your hearing instrument or implant in the left ear

17. How long do you use the current hearing aid in your left ear?

- ◯ Less than 6 weeks
- ◯ 6 weeks to 11 months
- ◯ 1 year to 10 years
- ◯ Over 10 years
- ◯ I have no hearing aid in my left ear

18. What is your total experience with the hearing aids, including all hearing instruments and implants that you ever had, in your left ear?

- ◯ Less than 6 weeks
- ◯ 6 weeks to 11 months
- ◯ 1 year to 10 years
- ◯ Over 10 years
- ◯ I have never had any hearing aid in my left ear

Questionnaire for people with hearing loss

Demographics

Demographics of people with the hearing loss

19. When did you realize you had hearing loss?

- ◯ At birth or before I learned to speak (prelingual hearing loss)
- ◯ After I learned to speak, but before I went to school
- ◯ During the primary, middle or high school
- ◯ During the study in the University, Institute, College, or Community College
- ◯ After I started to work

20. How much time did it take for you to resume your work after you got you first hearing aid?

- ◯ Less than a day
- ◯ More than a day but less than a week
- ◯ More than a week but less than a month
- ◯ More than a month but less than three months
- ◯ More than three months but less than six
- ◯ More than six months but less than a year
- ◯ More than a year
- ◯ When I got my first hearing aid I wasn't working
- ◯ I have never used a hearing aid

21. Indicate your age

- ◯ 0-17
- ◯ 18-34
- ◯ 35-44
- ◯ 45-54
- ◯ 55-64
- ◯ 65-74
- ◯ 75-84
- ◯ 85+

22. Indicate your gender

- ◯ Male
- ◯ Female

Questionnaire for people with hearing loss

23. Indicate the highest level of education you have completed

- ◯ Incomplete secondary education (Didn't graduate the school)
- ◯ Complete seconary education (Graduated high school)
- ◯ Incomplete professional education (Didn't graduate Vocational school or Community College, but studied)
- ◯ Complete professional education (Graduated Vocational school or Community College)
- ◯ Incomplete Higher Education (Didn't graduate University or College, but studied)
- ◯ Complete Higher Education (Graduated University or College)
- ◯ Other

24. Indicate your form of employment

- ◯ Full-time employment
- ◯ Part-time employment
- ◯ Retired
- ◯ Unemployed
- ◯ Housewife
- ◯ Disabled or not working due to poor health
- ◯ Entrepreneur or freelancer
- ◯ Other

25. Indicate the size of the human settlement (city, town, village etc.) where you live

- ◯ less than 50 thousand inhabitants
- ◯ from 50 thousand to 499 thousand inhabitants
- ◯ from 500 thousand to 1 million 999 thousand inhabitants
- ◯ more than 2 million inhabitants

26. Indicate the country of your residence

Country: [ ]

27. Indicate your marital status

- ◯ Married
- ◯ Widowed
- ◯ Divorced
- ◯ Has never been married
- ◯ Civil union

Questionnaire for people with hearing loss

Occupation

Data collection about occupation

28. What is your occupation?

29. What statements are true in your work life? Select all that applies

- ☐ I do a lot of manual labor
- ☐ I do very little or no manual labor at all
- ☐ I speak a lot over the phone
- ☐ I rarely speak over the phone
- ☐ Most of my working time I spend in the office
- ☐ I often speak one on one
- ☐ I often speak in groups
- ☐ I often have to speak in situations with a lot of background noise
- ☐ I rarely need to speak at my work
- ☐ I work on a computer most of my time
- ☐ I rarely work on a computer
- ☐ I have to speak often with new people
- ☐ Mostly, I speak only with people whom I know very well

30. What is your monthly household income?

- ○ less than 99 US Dollars
- ○ from 100 to 299 US Dollars
- ○ from 300 to 599 US Dollars
- ○ from 600 to 999 US Dollars
- ○ from 1000 to 1499 US Dollars
- ○ from 1500 to 1999 US Dollars
- ○ from 2000 to 2999 US Dollars
- ○ from 3000 to 3999 US Dollars
- ○ from 4000 to 4999 US Dollars
- ○ more than 5000 US Dollars

31. How many people in your household live on your montly household income?

Questionnaire for people with hearing loss

International Outcome Inventory for Hearing Aids

Questions on this page are the standard questionnaire IOI-HA (International Outcome Inventory for Hearing Aids). Our goal with these questions is to measure health outcomes of fitting with a hearing aid along the dimensions of Introspection and Interaction.

32. Think about how much you used your present hearing aid(s) over the past two weeks. On an average day, how many hours did you use the hearing aid(s)?

- ◯ None
- ◯ Less than 1 hour a day
- ◯ 1 to 4 hours a day
- ◯ 4 to 8 hours a day
- ◯ More than 8 hours a day

33. Think about the situation where you most wanted to hear better, before you got your present hearing aid(s). Over the past two weeks, how much has the hearing aid helped in that situation?

- ◯ Helped not at all
- ◯ Helped slightly
- ◯ Helped moderately
- ◯ Helped quite a lot
- ◯ Helped very much

34. Think again about the situation where you most wanted to hear better. When you use your present hearing aid(s), how much difficulty do you STILL have in that situation?

- ◯ Very much difficulty
- ◯ Quite a lot of difficulty
- ◯ Moderate difficulty
- ◯ Slight difficulty
- ◯ No difficulty

Questionnaire for people with hearing loss

35. Considering everything, do you think your present hearing aid(s) is worth the trouble?

- ◯ Not at all worth it
- ◯ Slightly worth it
- ◯ Moderately worth it
- ◯ Quite a lot worth it
- ◯ Very much worth it

36. Over the past two weeks, with your present hearing aid(s), how much have your hearing difficulties affected the things you can do?

- ◯ Affected very much
- ◯ Affected quite a lot
- ◯ Affected moderately
- ◯ Affected slightly
- ◯ Affected not at all

37. Over the past two weeks, with your present hearing aid(s), how much do you think other people were bothered by your hearing difficulties?

- ◯ Bothered very much
- ◯ Bothered quite a lot
- ◯ Bothered moderately
- ◯ Bothered slightly
- ◯ Bothered not at all

38. Considering everything, how much has your present hearing aid(s) changed your enjoyment of life?

- ◯ Worse
- ◯ No change
- ◯ Slightly better
- ◯ Quite a lot better
- ◯ Very much better

Questionnaire for people with hearing loss

Satisfaction with amplification in daily life

Questions on this page a part of the standart SADL (Satisfaction with amplification in daily life) questionnaire. The purpose of this questions is to measure health outcome along the dimensions of Positive Effect, Service & Cost, Negative Features, and Personal Image.

39. Compared to using no hearing aid at all, do your hearing aids help you understand the people you speak with most frequently?

- Not at all
- A little
- Somewhat
- Medium
- Considerably
- Greatly
- Tremendously

40. Are you frustrated when your hearing aids pick up sounds that keep you from hearing what you want to hear?

- Not at all
- A little
- Somewhat
- Medium
- Considerably
- Greatly
- Tremendously

41. Are you convinced that obtaining your hearing aids was in your best interests?

- Not at all
- A little
- Somewhat
- Medium
- Considerably
- Greatly
- Tremendously

Questionnaire for people with hearing loss

42. Do you think people notice your hearing loss more when you wear your hearing aids?

- ◯ Not at all
- ◯ A little
- ◯ Somewhat
- ◯ Medium
- ◯ Considerably
- ◯ Greatly
- ◯ Tremendously

43. Do your hearing aids reduce the number of times you have to ask people to repeat?

- ◯ Not at all
- ◯ A little
- ◯ Somewhat
- ◯ Medium
- ◯ Considerably
- ◯ Greatly
- ◯ Tremendously

44. Do you think your hearing aids are worth the trouble?

- ◯ Not at all
- ◯ A little
- ◯ Somewhat
- ◯ Medium
- ◯ Considerably
- ◯ Greatly
- ◯ Tremendously

Questionnaire for people with hearing loss

45. Are you bothered by an inability to get enough loudness from your hearing aids without feedback (whistling)?

- ○ Not at all
- ○ A little
- ○ Somewhat
- ○ Medium
- ○ Considerably
- ○ Greatly
- ○ Tremendously

46. How content are you with the appearance of your hearing aids?

- ○ Not at all
- ○ A little
- ○ Somewhat
- ○ Medium
- ○ Considerably
- ○ Greatly
- ○ Tremendously

47. Does wearing your hearing aids improve your self-confidence?

- ○ Not at all
- ○ A little
- ○ Somewhat
- ○ Medium
- ○ Considerably
- ○ Greatly
- ○ Tremendously

48. How natural is the sound from your hearing aids?

- ○ Not at all
- ○ A little
- ○ Somewhat
- ○ Medium
- ○ Considerably
- ○ Greatly
- ○ Tremendously

Questionnaire for people with hearing loss

49. How helpful are your hearing aids on MOST telephones with NO amplifier or loudspeaker?

- ◯ Not at all
- ◯ A little
- ◯ Somewhat
- ◯ Medium
- ◯ Considerably
- ◯ Greatly
- ◯ Tremendously

50. How competent was the person who provided you with your hearing aids?

- ◯ Not at all
- ◯ A little
- ◯ Somewhat
- ◯ Medium
- ◯ Considerably
- ◯ Greatly
- ◯ Tremendously
- ◯ I purchased my hearing aids on my own without any involvement of a hearing loss expert

51. Do you think wearing your hearing aids makes you seem less capable?

- ◯ Not at all
- ◯ A little
- ◯ Somewhat
- ◯ Medium
- ◯ Considerably
- ◯ Greatly
- ◯ Tremendously

Questionnaire for people with hearing loss

52. Does the cost of your hearing aids seem reasonable to you?

- Not at all
- A little
- Somewhat
- Medium
- Considerably
- Greatly
- Tremendously

53. How pleased are you with the dependability (how often they need repairs) of your hearing aids?

- Not at all
- A little
- Somewhat
- Medium
- Considerably
- Greatly
- Tremendously

Questionnaire for people with hearing loss

Hypothetical question

This question is classical in healthcare economics and will help us to understand better how much the unaided hearing loss impacts your enjoyment of life.

54. Imagine a situation: you are living the next 10 years with your current hearing loss but without the help of hearing aids. Now concentrate and try to estimate how many years of life with 100% hearing you consider equivalent to those 10 years.

- ○ 10
- ○ 9
- ○ 8
- ○ 7
- ○ 6
- ○ 5
- ○ 4
- ○ 3
- ○ 2
- ○ 1
- ○ 0

Questionnaire for people with hearing loss

Hypothetical scenario: treatment restoring hearing ability

This is another classical question in healthcare economics. The answer to this question will help us to assess your willingness to take a risk to improve your hearing ability.

55. Imagine a purely hypothetical situation: you come to see your doctor. To your surprise she has some interesting news for you. The doctor tells you that you have a unique type of hearing loss and there are no existing hearing aids that you could use to help you hear better. Besides, untreated, this hearing loss will lead you to death in around 10 years. But there is hope. They have an experimental free-of-charge treatment that, if successful, completely restores the hearing. The bad news is that in some cases it has severe side effects, even death can occur.
Thus you have only two options:
1. Reject the free-of-charge treatment course, and live another 10 years without hearing aids.
2. Take part in the treatment, which will either restore your hearing completely or make some major damage to your health including death.
Knowing all of the above, indicate the MINIMAL success rate of the treatment, which will make you consider taking a risk and undergoing the treatment.

- ○ 100%
- ○ 90%
- ○ 80%
- ○ 70%
- ○ 60%
- ○ 50%
- ○ 40%
- ○ 30%
- ○ 20%
- ○ 10%
- ○ 0%

Questionnaire for people with hearing loss

External help with the purchase of hearing aids

Information on the external help with the purchase of hearing instruments or implants

56. Indicate at what degree your health insurance covers the cost of your hearing aids

- I don't have health insurance
- I have health insurance, but it doesn't cover the cost of hearing aids I need
- I have health insurance, and it covers up to 10% of the cost of hearing aids
- I have health insurance, and it covers up to 30% of the cost of hearing aids
- I have health insurance, and it covers up to 50% of the cost of hearing aids
- I have health insurance, and it covers up to 70% of the cost of hearing aids
- I have health insurance, and it covers up to 100% of the cost of hearing aids

57. Indicate at what degree the government covers the cost of your hearing aids

- I'm not aware of any government help for purchase of hearing aids I need
- I know about the government help for purchase of hearing aids, but I am not qualified to receive its help
- I have the opportunity to receive the government help to buy hearing aids, and it covers up to 10% of their cost
- I have the opportunity to receive the government help to buy hearing aids, and it covers up to 30% of their cost
- I have the opportunity to receive the government help to buy hearing aids, and it covers up to 50% of their cost
- I have the opportunity to receive the government help to buy hearing aids, and it covers up to 70% of their cost
- I have the opportunity to receive the government help to buy hearing aids, and it covers up to 100% of their cost

58. Indicate at what degree the charity help covers the cost of your hearing aids

- I'm not aware of the existence of charity organizations that help with the purchase of hearing aids
- I know that charity organizations that help with the purchase of hearing aids exist, but I am not qualified to receive their help
- I have the opportunity to receive help from a charity organization, and it covers up to 10% of the cost of hearing aids
- I have the opportunity to receive help from a charity organization, and it covers up to 30% of the cost of hearing aids
- I have the opportunity to receive help from a charity organization, and it covers up to 50% of the cost of hearing aids
- I have the opportunity to receive help from a charity organization, and it covers up to 70% of the cost of hearing aids
- I have the opportunity to receive help from a charity organization, and it covers up to 100% of the cost of hearing aids

Questionnaire for people with hearing loss

59. Would you borrow money from your family members, relatives or friends to buy hearing aids you need?

- ◯ I would never borrow money from my family members, relatives or friends to buy hearing aids
- ◯ I would like to borrow money from my family members, relatives or friends to buy hearing aids, but I have no possibility to do so
- ◯ I would borrow up to 10% of the cost of hearing aids from my family members, relatives or friends
- ◯ I would borrow up to 30% of the cost of hearing aids from my family members, relatives or friends
- ◯ I would borrow up to 50% of the cost of hearing aids from my family members, relatives or friends
- ◯ I would borrow up to 70% of the cost of hearing aids from my family members, relatives or friends
- ◯ I would borrow up to 100% of the cost of hearing aids from my family members, relatives or friends

60. Would you borrow money from a bank or a credit union to buy hearing aids you need?

- ◯ I would never borrow money from a bank or a credit union to buy hearing aids
- ◯ I would like to borrow money from a bank or a credit union to buy hearing aids, but I have no possibility to do so
- ◯ I would borrow up to 10% of the cost of hearing aids from a bank or a credit union
- ◯ I would borrow up to 30% of the cost of hearing aids from a bank or a credit union
- ◯ I would borrow up to 50% of the cost of hearing aids from a bank or a credit union
- ◯ I would borrow up to 70% of the cost of hearing aids from a bank or a credit union
- ◯ I would borrow up to 100% of the cost of hearing aids from a bank or a credit union

Questionnaire for people with hearing loss

Savings

Questions on this page will help us to have a better understanding of your money saving ability, and analyse its influence on your ability to buy hearing aids that you need.

61. What money saving options do you usually use? Select all that applies

- ☐ I don't save money at all
- ☐ I save in cash at home or in an other place, but not in a bank
- ☐ I save in a bank
- ☐ I save with a credit union, microfinance organization or ROSCA (Rotating Savings and Credit Association)
- ☐ I save by buying property (such as appliances, cars, houses etc)
- ☐ I save in precious metals and/or stones (jewelry, gold, silver etc.)
- ☐ I save by investing in my own business or in the business of someone else
- ☐ I save by investing in my education

62. What would you prefer?

- ◯ To receive 200 US Dollars today
- ◯ To receive 250 US Dollars in one month

63. What would you prefer?

- ◯ To receive 200 US Dollars today
- ◯ To receive 300 US Dollars in one month

64. What would you prefer?

- ◯ To receive 200 US Dollars now
- ◯ To receive 350 US Dollars in one month

65. What would you prefer?

- ◯ To receive 200 US Dollars in 6 months
- ◯ To receive 250 US Dollars in 7 months

66. What would you prefer?

- ◯ To receive 200 US Dollars in 6 months
- ◯ To receive 300 US Dollars in 7 months

67. What would you prefer?

- ◯ To receive 200 US Dollars in 6 months
- ◯ To receive 350 US Dollars in 7 months

Questionnaire for people with hearing loss

Willingness to pay and the need in hearing aids

On this page we would try to estimate the gap between the need and the willingness to pay for the hearing aids. We would also consider possible ways to bridge the gap.

68. What price range includes hearing aids that you consider essential in order to integrate fully in the hearing society?

- ○ less than $100 US Dollars per hearing aid
- ○ from $101 US Dollars to $300 US Dollars per hearing aid
- ○ from $301 US Dollars to $500 US Dollars per hearing aid
- ○ from $501 US Dollars to $800 US Dollars per hearing aid
- ○ from $801 US Dollars to $1100 US Dollars per hearing aid
- ○ from $1101 US Dollars to $1500 US Dollars per hearing aid
- ○ from $1501 US Dollars to $2000 US Dollars per hearing aid
- ○ from $2001 US Dollars to $3000 US Dollars per hearing aid
- ○ more than $3001 US Dollars per hearing aid

69. How much money can you afford to spend on hearing aids?

- ○ less than $100 US Dollars per hearing aid
- ○ less than $300 US Dollars per hearing aid
- ○ less than $500 US Dollars per hearing aid
- ○ less than $800 US Dollars per hearing aid
- ○ less than $1100 US Dollars per hearing aid
- ○ less than $1500 US Dollars per hearing aid
- ○ less than $2000 US Dollars per hearing aid
- ○ less than $3000 US Dollars per hearing aid
- ○ more than $3001 US Dollars per hearing aid

Questionnaire for people with hearing loss

70. What would you recommend your friend, who has the same hearing loss like you do, but cannot afford to buy hearing aids right now? Select everything that applies

- [ ] To take a loan in a bank, credit union or in another credit organization
- [ ] To borrow the money from friends, family or relatives
- [ ] To save the money for the purchase on a bank account
- [ ] To save the money in cash (at home or in the other place, but not in a bank, credit union or another credit organization)
- [ ] To sell some of his belongings, appliances or property in order to get the money to buy the hearing aid(s)
- [ ] To buy the hearing aids that he can afford right now without any loans
- [ ] Not to buy hearing aids at all, because they don't help
- [ ] Not to buy hearing aids at all, because you know how to get them for free (government program etc)

A-2: Adjustment of the Income Level

The starting point of the income level calculation is the answer to the question #30 "What is your monthly household income?". This answer is adjusted using the following variables:

- question #31 "How many people in your household live on your monthly household income";
- question #25 "Indicate the size of the human settlement (city, town, village etc.) where you live";
- question #26 "Indicate the country of your residence".

The logic behind the adjustment is the following:

- Household income adjustment either makes no changes or decreases the hearing impaired person's income;
- The lowest hearing impaired person's income is "less than 99 US Dollars" (the lowest income bracket in the income list for the question #30);
- An average of the income bracket is taken for deduction of additional household member costs;
- If a hearing impaired person lives in a city with less than 2 million people inhabitants in Ukraine or other low income country; less than 500 thousand inhabitants in Russia or other middle income country; or less than 50 thousand inhabitants in the USA or other developed country, then for each member of household living with the hearing impaired USD 200 is deducted per month;
- If a hearing impaired person lives in a city with more than 2 million people inhabitabts in Ukraine or other low income country; more than 500 thousand inhabitants, but less than 2 million people in Russia or other middle income country; or less than 500 thousand inhabitants, but more than 50 thousand people in the USA or other developed country, then for each member of household living with the hearing impaired USD 300 is deducted per month;
- If a hearing impaired person lives in a city with more than 2 million people inhabitabts in Russia or other middle income country; or less than 2 million inhabitants, but more than 500 thousand people in the USA or other developed country, then for each member of household living with the hearing impaired USD 400 is deducted per month;

- If a hearing impaired person lives in a city with more than 2 million people inhabitabts in the USA or other developed country, then for each member of household living with the hearing impaired USD 500 is deducted per month.

The result of such an adjustment is used in this research as a hearing impaired person's income.

MIX
Papier aus verantwortungsvollen Quellen
Paper from responsible sources
FSC® C105338

If you have any concerns about our products,
you can contact us on
ProductSafety@springernature.com

In case Publisher is established outside the EU,
the EU authorized representative is:
Springer Nature Customer Service Center GmbH
Europaplatz 3, 69115 Heidelberg, Germany

Printed by Libri Plureos GmbH
in Hamburg, Germany